HILDEGARD OF BINGEN

Books by Matthew Fox

The Pope's War: Why Ratzinger's Secret Crusade Has Imperiled the Church and What Can Be Saved

Christian Mystics: 365 Readings and Meditations

The Hidden Spirituality of Men: Ten Metaphors to Awaken the Sacred Masculine

The A.W.E. Project: Reinventing Education, Reinventing the Human

A New Reformation: Creation Spirituality & the Transformation of Christianity

Creativity: Where the Divine and the Human Meet

Prayer: A Radical Response to Life 2001,
(formerly *On Becoming a Musical, Mystical Bear*)

One River, Many Wells: Wisdom Springing From Global Faiths 2000

Sins of the Spirit, Blessings of the Flesh:
Lessons for Transforming Evil in Soul and Society

The Physics of Angels – with biologist Rupert Sheldrake

Natural Grace – with biologist Rupert Sheldrake

Passion for Creation, The Earth-Honoring Spirituality of Meister Eckhart
(formerly *Breakthrough*)

Wrestling With the Prophets: Essays on Creation Spirituality and Everyday Life

The Reinvention of Work: A New Vision of Livelihood For Our Time

Sheer Joy: Conversations with Thomas Aquinas on Creation Spirituality

Creation Spirituality: Liberating Gifts for the Peoples of the Earth

The Coming of the Cosmic Christ: The Healing of Mother Earth and The Birth of Illuminations of Hildegard of Bingen

Original Blessing: A Primer in Creation Spirituality

Meditations with Meister Eckhart

A Spirituality Named Compassion

Confessions: The Making of a Post-Denominational Priest

Hildegard of Bingen's Book of Divine Works, Songs & Letters

Whee! We, Wee All the Way Home: A Guide to Sensual, Prophetic Spirituality

Religion USA: Religion and Culture by way of *TIME Magazine*

Manifesto for a Global Civilization (with Brian Swimme)

Passion for Creation: Meister Eckhart's Creation Spirituality

In the Beginning There Was Joy (children's book, illustrated)

Western Spirituality: Historical Roots, Ecumenical Routes, editor

HILDEGARD
of Bingen
A SAINT FOR OUR TIMES

UNLEASHING HER POWER
IN THE 21ST CENTURY

Matthew Fox

namaste
PUBLISHING

Vancouver, Canada

Library and Archives Canada Cataloguing in Publication

Fox, Matthew, 1940-
    Hildegard of Bingen : a saint for our times : unleashing her
power in the 21st century/ Matthew Fox.

Includes bibliographical references.
ISBN 978-1-897238-73-8

    1. Hildegard, Saint, 1098-1179. 2. Christian saints--Germany--
Biography. I. Title.

BX4700.H5F69 2012   282.092   C2012-904728-7

Published in Canada by
Namaste Publishing
P. O. Box 62084
Vancouver, British Columbia V6J 4A3
www.namastepublishing.com

Distributed in North America by PGW, Berkeley, CA USA
Typesetting by Steve Amarillo, Urban Design LLC
Cover Design by Diane McIntosh

Printed and bound in Canada by Friesens

MIX
Paper from
responsible sources
FSC
www.fsc.org   FSC® C016245

Dedication

To all those women and men who have committed
themselves to reversing the patriarchal consciousness
that has dominated humanity for so long by heralding
the return of the Divine Feminine and the healthy
masculine—and by so doing, daring to challenge
the entrenched status quo.

Contents

Foreword

Somewhere there hangs a poster that reads, "Those who have lived well for their own time have lived well for all times." At one stage of human development, this can be a difficult concept to understand. After all, there is one thing of which we are unequivocally certain: we live once. Only once. We live in our own times, shaped by our own times, and constrained by our own times. Beyond that, most of us have little or no aspirations. After all, it is enough to have done that well, isn't it? For what else can we possibly hope?

But then comes the stage of life when we finally begin to realize how short life really is. Then, too often surely, the question becomes what, in the long view of life, so small a moment in time can possibly mean? After all, we know that the scope of the average human being is limited and that the very thought of producing something that might live on beyond us has the ring of absurdity to it. Few monuments of the past still stand. Few of anyone's words live on. Few of the world's ancient accomplishments serve us still. The aqueducts are gone, the walls are down, the books are out of print, the spears have dulled with rust.

Echoes of those questions haunt us, pursue us through time, shape our sense of purpose, confront the very soul of us.

Shelley's sonnet "Ozymandias" appeared in England in the early 19th century, at the beginning of the industrial age when newness was becoming an addiction. The monarchies are falling then, the steamships are on the water, the light bulb has been lit. The unheard of seems possible. Everything old is being scorned now, and even the best things the age had produced—the ornate carriages, the awesome dynasties, the cavalries, the oil lamps—were fast becoming relics. And in the center of it all, the poet Shelley sounds a warning for all to hear. He writes of the broke and toppled statue of a great pharaoh found in the Egyptian desert and says:

> On the pedestal these words appear
> "My name is Ozymandias, king of kings:
> Look on my works, ye Mighty, and despair!"
> Nothing beside remains. Round the decay
> Of that colossal wreck, boundless and bare
> The lone and level sands stretch far away.

The message is ominously clear: everything passes away, nothing is permanent, no power is absolute, no reign lasts, nothing we do really matters.

At first glance, the words seem wise, seem weighted with truth. But at another stage of life, the words take on an aura of the simplistic. As a matter of fact, we come to know that it isn't true that nothing lasts. On the contrary, everything lasts. Everything matters. Everything we do counts. Everything is prelude, stepping stone, and promise. The only thing any age needs to become the next one is someone with the courage to challenge the past, to embody the future, to announce its reality, and to cope with the demand that transition brings.

If ever we need to be reminded of the effect of one age on another, of the impact of even one figure on the world, this clear, creative, insightful book is certainly proof of it.

Hildegard of Bingen was born almost 1,000 years ago! But in this book she lives again in our time. In this book, it's easy to see how she proclaimed our coming simply by refusing to accept in her time what we are still trying to achieve in ours. She gave us both the permission to trust our own insights and the call to require them for the women who will come after us. What she knew then, our best thinkers are calling us to now.

This book doesn't look at Hildegard of Bingen as an icon of an age long gone by. This book looks at Hildegard as harbinger, prophet, template of our own. This book doesn't sink us into the past; it requires us to analyze our own role in the present with all of her gifts in mind. It links the acts and insights of the past to the ongoing agendas of our own age.

The theological insights Hildegard brought to the 11th century stretched the spiritual viewpoint of the church beyond the legal to the moral.

The ethical concerns Hildegard raised in both church and state still underlie the hopes in this age for a church that demonstrates more compassion for those who suffer than for the canonical niceties that condemn them.

The intellectual gifts she gave to the world totally unbidden confirm the desires of the women of our own time to be contributing thinkers to our own world, bidden or not, welcome or not.

The vision of "the web of life" that Hildegard gave her time challenges our own sense of planetary citizenship.

The regard, respect, and religious repute she brought to the place of science in the spiritual life brought religion beyond the magical to the mystical.

The figure of Hildegard herself as woman—bright, bold, fearless, and confident of her place in God's creation, of woman's place in the image of God—gives heart to women still beaten, rebuffed, sold, enslaved, and ignored in our own.

This is Hildegard of Bingen, Doctor of the Church, a woman for all women to find in themselves, to follow and to proclaim as sign and model of what they themselves must be permitted to be.

What Hildegard did counted then and counts still. And so must we.

Read this book with these words ringing in your soul: "The purpose of life," the essayist Rosten writes, "is not to be happy. The purpose of life is to matter; to have it make a difference that you lived at all."

This book gives strong, sterling, and unvarnished evidence that everything—everything—we ourselves become will affect what women after us may also become. For their sakes, take heart from this great woman, learn from her, be strengthened by her, and live life in such a way yourself that makes a difference for those who will come after you.

This is a truly marvelous, useful, profound, and creative book.

Joan Chittister, OSB

Introduction

HILDEGARD OF BINGEN

Herald of the Divine Feminine, Green Prophet, Church Reformer

I heard a voice speaking to me: 'The young woman whom you see is Love. She has her tent in eternity... It was love which was the source of this creation in the beginning when God said: 'Let it be!' And it was. As though in the blinking of an eye, the whole creation was formed through love. The young woman is radiant in such a clear, lightning-like brilliance of countenance that you can't fully look at her... She holds the sun and moon in her right hand and embraces them tenderly... The whole of creation calls this maiden 'Lady.' For it was from her that all of creation proceeded, since Love was the first. She made everything... Love was in eternity and brought forth, in the beginning of all holiness, all creatures without any admixture of evil. Adam and Eve, as well were produced by love from the pure nature of the Earth.

–Hildegard[1]

One of the greatest honors a person can receive in the Roman Catholic Church is to be declared not only a saint, but also a Doctor of the Church. The Canonization of Hildegard of Bingen in October, 2012, by Pope Benedict XVI, is a landmark in more ways than one. Not only is she only the fourth woman in history to be declared a Doctor of the Church—joining the names of Catherine of Siena, St Teresa of Avila, and St Therese of Lisieux—but her recognition in this way seems ironic for many reasons.

The rules of canonization were radically altered under the papacy of John Paul II, when the role of the "devil's advocate" was removed from the canonization process. This opened the door to the possibility that practically anyone could qualify for canonization if they had the financial backing and inside connections to see it through.

Nevertheless, canonization and the title of "Doctor of the Church" do carry still some archetypal power. Hildegard's canonization and elevation as a Doctor of the Church comes at a significant moment in the history of both our planet and the church. While canonization may not be worth as much in itself these days, Hildegard's is fundamentally different. She is what we expect a saint to be: a mover and a shaker, a force to be dealt with not only in her day but also in ours, a bold and courageous human being to be listened to and emulated.

Hildegard's message is remarkably on target for our era—over eight centuries after her passing! In this 21st century, when time is running out for our species unless we make drastic changes to how we function on this planet, Hildegard's voice is sorely needed, for she speaks to the core issues that are ushering us down the path to oblivion.

In the first place, Hildegard calls for a marriage of science and spirituality. For religion and the secular sciences to be sundered as they currently are is a blunder of immense proportions on the part of our species—and with potentially dire consequences. Hildegard calls upon us to employ our intellect, which she names "our greatest treasure," as well as our mystical intuition. She calls for a move from a mere quest for knowledge, with the power it bestows, to a revival of wisdom. She calls for an awakening of the kind of creativity she refers to as "greening power," leading to an honoring of Mother Earth and the return of the Green Man to replace the destruction of the environment that's occurring apace in our technologically and industrially-oriented era. The term "Green Man" refers to an archetype that underscores the deep relationship between the human and the plant world, the human and the natural world.

At a time when traditionally the most loyal followers of Catholicism—the sisters of the church—are being chastised by the Vatican for their involvement in issues of social justice, the environment, the assertion of the feminine voice and viewpoint, and the freedom to make one's own choices of conscience before God rather than mindlessly bowing to the will of an all-male ecclesia, Hildegard calls for the emergence of the Divine Feminine to balance a healthy Sacred Masculine.

When those who seek nothing more than to *be the church*, recognizing that the church isn't only the Vatican, the princes of the church, and the bishops, but *every* member of the church—a truth articulated by the Second Vatican Council—Hildegard calls upon us to find the "strength" that spiritual warriors all require. The Second Vatican Council was a worldwide gathering of bishops and theologians called by Pope John XXIII in 1962 to "open the windows" of the Catholic Church and bring about a religious reform and awakening by rehabilitating some of its most progressive thinkers who had been sidelined for decades by too much legalism in the church. One of its declarations was that the church is "the people of God," not just the hierarchy. It is in the spirit of Vatican II that Hildegard stresses that it isn't only the leadership, but the rank and file who are called to be the church. Being the warrior that she is, Hildegard stands up to corruption and patriarchy wherever she sees it—in religion, in government, in all places of power—and she invites us to do the same. She is a woman for our time, a teacher for our time, a Doctor and a saint for our time.

Is it not remarkable that, at this moment when the Vatican seeks to silence the nuns and the theologians who want only to fulfill the work given to them by Vatican II, a woman whom the church has been largely silent about all these centuries is now brought to the fore as an example of sainthood—a woman whose teaching and preaching (yes, she was allowed to preach!) is a virtual earthquake to the establishment today, as it was in her own time?

Even today, despite all our progress, denial of the feminine is so pervasive that anthropologist Glenn Hughes says a male terror of women is woven into every institution. It's this denial of the feminine that's destroying the ecosphere. Mother Earth, like her human daughters, has become an object to be used. Such patriarchal excess is found in all fundamentalism, whether the Vatican, the Taliban, or Pat Robertson.

In our time the Divine Feminine is returning in the awakening of women the world over to their rights, as well as to their common suffering and abuse, no less than in the many experiences believers and non-believers alike are undergoing with visitations from the Black Madonna, for example. Or the return of Sophia, Wisdom, and the role of the Brown Madonna—the Lady of Guadalupe—and other archetypes of the Divine Feminine that are also coming alive in appeals to defend Gaia, our Earth Mother, after centuries of rape and plunder.

Hildegard understood the importance of the restoration of women's deeply buried, culturally obscured feminine wisdom. She recognized that when women come into their own, there will be an end to the power-over dynamics that have blighted the planet. Only the integration of a healthy Sacred Masculine and a resurrected Divine Feminine can save us from our destructive ways.

In line with this insight, Hildegard asks us to love our bodies—indeed, to *love life itself*, which she equates with God. Her theology is built on experience of the divine, which is to say on mysticism. The experience she most espouses is that of God in creation—in other words the Cosmic Christ, which is the God-presence in every being in the universe—and/or "Lady Wisdom." She calls for an expansion of consciousness that a renewed cosmology can bring and asks that we look not just at human agendas but also at the universe itself for delight, warmth, and rules to live by.

In short, Hildegard is a timely *herald* of good news to the tired souls of the earth, resurrected from obscurity against all odds in light of the patriarchal crackdown of the present Vatican—surely testimony to the work of the Spirit deep in the unconscious of humankind. Is it not a miracle that, when her voice is so needed, Hildegard speaks to us afresh despite almost nine centuries of virtual obscurity?

I want to emphasize Hildegard's role as a "herald." Webster's dictionary defines the work of "heralding" as "to give notice of," "to announce," or "to greet with enthusiasm." I believe Hildegard does all this as a herald of the Divine Feminine. She gives notice, announces, and greets with enthusiasm. In so doing, she points the way to an alternative to the fundamentalism that's raging the world over—from the Christian Bible belt to the fundamentalism in the Vatican, Islam, Judaism, Hinduism, and wherever patriarchy feels threatened.

The late and great Christian monk Father Bede Griffiths, who directed an ashram in southern India that honored both Hindu and Christian ways for over fifty years, wrote that "the disastrous effects of Western industrialism, physical, social and psychological, polluting the world and threatening to destroy it are only too evident." But the cause is "due to a fundamental defect in Western man," which is the excessive rationalism and masculine "dominating power of the mind" that needs to be balanced by the feminine, intuitive, receptive power of the mind.[2]

Father Griffiths believed that the East has much to teach the West about regaining a balance of masculine-feminine, yang-yin energies. "The suppression of women in the Church is but one of the many signs of this masculine domination... Reason has to be 'married' to intuition; it has to learn to surrender itself for the deeper intuitions of the spirit. These intuitions come, as we have seen, from the presence of the Spirit in the depths of the soul."[3] Hildegard takes us to these depths. She takes us beyond the domination of the rational masculine, even while she praises the use of rationality and intellect. In short, she takes us to a place where the Divine Feminine is welcomed once again.

The purpose of this book is to make Hildegard's message available, and to do so employing her words as much as possible—for nothing touches so deeply as Hildegard in her own words. In the course of writing this book, something quite unexpected happened to me (surprises often happen when I'm writing a book, which means that one reason for my writing is to learn something new and be surprised). I realized how eager Hildegard was to "mix," a postmodern thing to do, and dialog with contemporary thinkers such as Mary Oliver, Albert Einstein, Howard Thurman, Clarissa Pinkola Estes, Dorothee Soelle, and other voices of wisdom—including, of course, Jesus and the Buddha. I'm happy to introduce Hildegard to these people. Her powerful work deserves to be integrated with other movers and shakers whose work affects us all.

Something happens when you read Hildegard. I know this because I've been living with her for over thirty years and teaching her for more than twenty-eight years. Something also happens when you listen to Hildegard's music—and even more so if you sing her music. Further, something happens when you meditate on her visions, her mandalas, her paintings. I know because I've been touched deeply by her words, her music, her paintings, and her story.

Recently I conducted a retreat based on Hildegard's work, and the energy released by those who came in contact with her was both beautiful and powerful. Over the years of sharing her wisdom, I've listened to many stories of individuals who have been touched and awakened by Hildegard entering their life. There's an uncanny power in the beauty and strength—even the urgency--of her language and her teachings.

This book intends to explore some of those teachings that seem most pertinent and pressing for our time—an era, as we are all aware, of challenge and peril for Mother Earth and her creatures, and for the human race and its efforts in such areas of culture as religion, economics, education, and politics.

It's my conviction that behind the canonization of Hildegard and the declaration that she is now a "Doctor of the Church" lies a deep and demanding truth—*that if we dare honor her, we ought also to listen to her with open hearts and minds.* For she calls us today to deep reform of church corruption and spiritual "lukewarmness," to use her word. She also awakens us to the perils generated by a culture still dominated by patriarchal structures and values—values that put profit and power for a few ahead of the needs of all for healthy bodies, minds, spirits, communities, and the planet itself. Structures that put dominance ahead of partnership.

Hildegard's main theme is that we should "wake up." This is every true spiritual teacher's main theme. For instance, Jesus said, "The kingdom of God is among you," which implies we better wake up and experience it. Buddha means "the awakened one," and he invited everyone to be a "light unto yourself." Waking up is the opposite of denial. Hildegard dares us to move beyond denial.

I just took a walk along the water's edge, and the jasmine trees were pouring forth their amazing scent, the birds were singing their memorable songs, the waters were glistening, and the ducks were coming out for the evening ritual of sunset. My awareness of nature's aliveness and greening power was increased by spending time with Hildegard, for she sensitizes one's senses, awakening them—just like the "Word" that she writes so convincingly and intimately about.

In a similar manner, on a Sunday morning, in the wee hours while darkness still lay over all, I awoke to a single bird singing a unique song outside my window. I had never heard such a song from a bird before. I listened intently to understand this birdsong. After a while the singing stopped and all was quiet as night once again. The song, I swear, was this: "Thank you, thank you, thank you, thank you." It sounded on and on. Hours later, when the sun was rising, other birds started up their own more familiar melodies.

What was this? Was it Hildegard visiting me once again? Was it her Rhineland mystic companions—Eckhart, Aquinas, Julian, and Mecthild—also serenading me as I write about them too? I would like to think so. Yes, I would. I have never thought this thought before—that maybe this work pleases them (if not so many of my contemporaries, and *especially* not those running patriarchal religious establishments!). Perhaps they are thanking me, just as I try through my work to thank them and to bring them into our time when they are so *needed.* Hildegard wrote in a letter composed late in her life to her Benedictine sisters, "I want to be useful." Well, you *are* useful Hildegard. You are *very* useful today.

That is the point of this book—to render Hildegard useful. To take her off library shelves and out of academic paper contests into the hearts and souls of people and their dying, mordant, dry, and ungreen institutions, whether school, church, economics, politics, or the media. To give her the wings to challenge Wall Street, the Vatican, and the self-serving political machines of patriarchal plutocracy that are destroying the planet in this 21st century, just as she exposed religious hypocrisy and unjust social structures in the 12th century, warning of the dark results of greed and self-serving actions, including the despoiling of the earth.

I want to say, "You were a prophet then, Hildegard, and you are a prophet today. Come and bring some of your feminist dynamism alive again in our tired, cynical, military-ridden, self-pitying world—a world that patriarchy built. Yes, help us to allow the Divine Feminine to flow again—and with it a healthy, not perverse, Sacred Masculine." As Sister Joan Chittister, a direct descendant of Hildegard in the Benedictine tradition, says, the issue today is not "radical feminism," which the Vatican accuses Catholic sisters in America of, but "radical patriarchy." I couldn't agree more. Recovering a healthy Sacred Masculine is so important if we are to deconstruct the reptilian brain and the testosterone-induced, patriarchal, dominator consciousness that's a danger for women, men, and the planet itself.

To this end I wrote a book a few years ago called *The Hidden Spirituality of Men: Ten Metaphors for Awakening the Sacred Masculine.* In addition to dealing with ten healthy male archetypes, I ended it with two chapters on the "sacred marriage" of the Divine Feminine and Sacred Masculine.[4] I've come to realize that in many ways the present book is a continuation of that book. For this present book, thanks to Hildegard's life and work, takes us all deeper into a healthy Divine Feminine, not at the expense of the Sacred Masculine but in consort with it.

Two responses to my "men's book" seem relevant here. The first response I received was from a woman who said, "I have over 200 books on the goddess in my personal library and not one book on the Sacred Masculine. Yet I have three boys! I have been so busy coming into my spiritual womanhood that I had no idea what men have suffered under Patriarchy until I read your book."

A second response came from an elegantly dressed Native American elder with long silver hair, who approached me after a talk at a conference in Santa Fe. "I have been working in prisons for twelve years," he said, "and I have never had the results with a book like I have had with your book. Prisoners are invariably projecting onto others, but your book is the first I have ever employed that *gets men in touch with their own nobility.*" Isn't this what all spirituality is meant to do? Isn't it what Hildegard is telling us in the beautiful vision with which I opened this introduction? The balance of a healthy feminine and a healthy masculine within both men and women—for we all carry both within us—is essential for the survival of our species. And Hildegard leads the way.

In this book, I want to emphasize *experience,* for Hildegard emphasizes experience—and experience is what's so often lacking in narcissistic religion and overly institutionalized "churchiness." Experience is what distinguishes spirituality from religion. Spirituality is about experience—and it's those poets of experience, the mystics, who can and must revitalize religion for us.

Hildegard is such a person. Just reading her words can trigger experiences in one's soul that awaken, refresh, and empower. So this book is hopefully a chalice by which Hildegard's words can shower down upon us, refreshing us and enlivening us, and above all *putting us in touch with our experience of the divine.*

Divinity isn't something to be argued about or defined in our pretty little boxes of denominationalism. Neither is it something to accept or reject, let alone to go to war over. Divinity is beyond all names, as

Meister Eckhart put it, a "superessential darkness that has no name and will never be given a name."

We could say that divinity is our *experience of the depths of life,* such as are laid out in the four paths of creation spirituality, which we will come to in chapter 6. "Taste and see that God is good," says the psalmist. Hildegard is one who tasted, and tasted deeply. That's the basis of wisdom—a tasting. Indeed, the words for wisdom in both Hebrew and Latin come from the word "to taste."

One of Hildegard's special teachings is that we are all born in "original wisdom," to quote her words. But we are tiny babes in our mother's womb, and wisdom comes as a folded tent inside us. Life's journey consists of setting up this tent. Hildegard draws pictures of this, and the journey isn't easy. Our souls traverse valleys and mountains, ford rivers, and meet opposition all along the route. But Hildegard pictures the tent of wisdom eventually set up and angels warding off the dark forces that attack us still.

Hildegard derives her inspiration for this teaching from the Hebrew Bible, where we are told that Wisdom wandered the earth seeking where to set up her tent. John's Gospel tells us Wisdom set up her tent in Christ. "Set it up here," says Hildegard, "in each and every soul, each and everyone's life journey." We are born in wisdom, but it's our life's task to develop this wisdom and practice and put it to work.

In this book we'll explore the richness of Hildegard's writings by examining favorite concepts and categories in her thought. We'll also examine her lineage, the creation spiritual tradition that she was both heir to and also leader of in her own unique right—and for which reason I call her the "grandmother" of the Rhineland mystic movement.

Thomas Aquinas instructs us that for teaching spirituality, experience isn't sufficient—though it's essential. One also needs concepts. Thus we will explore the basic concepts that hold and nourish Hildegard's teachings and visions—concepts that shed light on own journeys. An Appendix presents spiritual practices we can undertake in the spirit of Hildegard to strengthen our courage and steadfastness on the journey.

This is a short book and deliberately so. Even so, I hope you'll find it neither superficial nor without inspiration. It's meant for ordinary people, busy people, people on the go who seek some timeless wisdom from a past that yearns to speak to us today in the midst of our personal, cultural, and planetary turbulence—wisdom that gives perspective to our existence.

Hildegard was a woman of profundity and of intense inspiration. In poet Mary Oliver's language, she didn't just "pass through" her time on earth. On the contrary, her 81 years vibrated with so much creativity and expansion of consciousness that she calls to us still, over 800 years later, to "rise from our sleep" and "live with passion and blood," in order that we might contribute to "making the cosmic wheel go around."

Journey with me in these pages as Hildegard speaks to us from her deep wisdom, large heart, and genius intelligence. Let us hear her voice from the renaissance of the 12th century, as she calls to the current void of the 21st century. Out of the void, a rebirth of spirituality can come— indeed, a new and global renaissance that's so needed. Out of the *emergency* in which we find ourselves as a species, there can *emerge* an intelligent, ecumenical, justice-oriented, scientifically respectful, creative, green spirituality.

This is my third book on Hildegard, and in the years since I first began traveling with her, much in culture and spirituality has evolved. In my most recent book, *The Pope's War*, I lay out the case for recognizing how the Vatican itself has been in schism for forty years because it has betrayed the principles of the Second Vatican Council. Hildegard railed against popes, bishops, abbots, and priests of her day who were silent in the face of schism or were partners in the corruption of the church. What would she say to the pedophile horrors and cover-ups of our time? What would she say to the attacks on theologians and the heretical teaching that the magisterium of the church is the Vatican alone? What would she say to the five Roman Catholic supreme court judges who declared that corporations are people, and thus opened the floodgates for billionaires and corporations to dominate what was once a democracy? What would she do to arouse people out of denial and into action? As you will read below, Hildegard didn't mince her words when justice and injustice were involved. She spoke with the authority of the Spirit at work through her. She spoke in words as vivid today as they were in her time.

Prophets like Hildegard return from time to time to assist us. She is a Bodhisattva in our midst. Listen to her as she speaks your name.

Matthew Fox
Friends of Creation Spirituality and Academy of the Love of Learning
September, 2012

Chapter 1

WHO IS HILDEGARD?

Who is this woman who sang that "all of creation is a symphony of joy and jubilation"?

Who is this woman who got herself and her entire abbey interdicted—a kind of group excommunication—by the archbishop for a full year when she was eighty years old?

Who is this woman who saw in a vision that a young and beautiful woman is responsible for all of creation, and her name is Love—and that all creation is based on Love and is therefore an Original Blessing?

Who is this woman who preached of the "web of life" that all creation shares, but who warned that "the earth must not be injured, the earth must not be destroyed"—and that if humans misuse creation, "God will permit creation to punish humanity"?

Who is this woman who calls Christ a "green man" in the century in which the Green Man entered Western culture riding on the coattails of the returning goddess?

Who is this woman who calls us all "co-creators" with God?

Who is this woman whom scholars recognize as "the only known female systematic exegete of the Middle Ages"?[1]

Who is this woman who developed a theology of the Holy Spirit, who reaches all of our lives through creativity and greening power, and "fills all things with interconnectivity and interrelationship," more than eight centuries before postmodern scientists began to say the same?

Who is this woman who developed in depth a theology of the Cosmic Christ eight centuries before Teilhard de Chardin?

Who is this woman who said that "all science is a gift from God" and that "your greatest treasure is your regal intellect," in the face of anti-intellectual fundamentalists of her day and ours?

Who is this woman whose teachings on healing and medicine are so useful even today that a clinic in Germany has employed them for over thirty years with considerable success?

Who is this woman who taught how we should all "search out the house of wisdom" in our hearts before all else?

Who is this woman who talked about an "original wisdom" that we are all born into, in the midst of a pessimistic theological tradition that had been preaching "original sin" for the previous 800 years—an idea proposed in the fourth century by St Augustine?

Who is this woman who celebrated the union of creativity and wisdom when she declared that "wisdom is found in all creative works," thereby giving us a model by which to reinvent education itself?

Who is this woman who built her theology on Lady Wisdom, Sophia, the Divine Feminine, and who declared that Mary is "the ground of all being," just like the goddesses of old?

Who is this woman who called the serpent "the wisest of all creatures," when the serpent is the ancient symbol of the goddess, whose story took an abusive direction when patriarchy destroyed the goddess civilizations?

Who is this woman who declared that redemption occurs through the *incarnation*, not pinning it entirely on the crucifixion?

Who is this woman who painted Adam as a red man?

Who is this woman who paints Christ as coming *from below* the earth, from under the earth—and from the lower chakras, not the head chakras?

Who is this woman who painted Christ as a blue man, "the man in sapphire blue," who is the healing presence inside all of us and whose primary work is compassion?

Who is this woman who celebrated eros and proposed that Adam's fall was a failure of eros—a failure to take delight in the beauty and grace of creation, and that we can fall in the same way?

Who is this woman who tells us God and creation are related like husband to wife, and like lovers to one another—and that an erotic "kiss" binds them together?

Who is this woman who stated that "holy people draw to themselves all that is earthy"?

Who is this woman whom the 20th century eco-prophet Thomas Berry says offered a "third model" of human relationship with the natural world—one based on a model of the earth "as a region of delight," indeed "a pagan delight," who "sees the creation-maker in the ancient manner of the fertility cults... Because of this 'erotic' bond the earth becomes luxuriant in its every aspect?"[2]

Who is this woman who had visions from the time she was five years old, and as an adult painted thirty-six of her visions, many in mandala form, and commented on them?

Who is this German woman who includes Hopi corn mothers in her paintings?

Who is this woman who invented the first "full-fledged morality play"?

Who is this woman who heard angels singing and put the sounds to music?

Who is this woman who wrote the first opera of the West, 300 years before any other?

Who is this woman who composed music that anticipated Mozart and Haydn by 600 years, since she deployed thematic development and themes that move in and out of her songs?

Who is this woman whose music takes one to ever deeper and loftier realms of divine experience?

Who is this woman who brings alive again the person and teachings of Jesus—and does so with music, poetry, theology, opera, medicine, letters, paintings, and yoga-like ecstatic experiences of soul and body that occur while singing her demanding music?

Who is this woman who taught that the only sin is "drying up," and wrote abbots and bishops telling them to abandon their dryness, get out of their buildings, and do whatever it took to get "wet and green and moist and juicy"?

Who is this woman who, ironically, is being declared a "saint" and a "Doctor of the Church" by a papacy that denounces women's rights and makes war on Catholic sisters—and even girl scouts—in America, and on thinking theologians on five continents?

Who is this woman who called Rome "evil" 400 years before Luther and the Protestant Reformers, and 900 years before the schismatic papacies of John Paul II and Benedict XVI abandoned the reforms and principles of the Second Vatican Council to persecute the base communities of Latin America and condemn theologians for doing their job, which is to think?[3]

Who is this woman who wrote popes telling them that they "silently tolerated corrupt men," and thus threw "the whole world in confusion" 900 years before the truth came out about Pope John Paul II allowing sexual predators to occupy the priesthood and oversee religious orders while abusing seminarians? And with Cardinal Ratzinger, now Pope, as head of the Congregation of the Doctrine of the Faith, saying such a man—Father Maciel—mustn't be ejected because he had "done so much good for the church"?

Who is this woman who constantly calls the papacy back to doing justice and admonishes the pope, "You, O Rome, are like one in the throes of death. You will be so shaken that the strength of your feet, the feet on which you now stand, will disappear. For you don't love the King's daughter, Justice"?

Who is this woman who wrote the pope that he was surrounded by men "who bark like dogs and make stupid sounds like chickens, which sometimes begin to cackle in the middle of the night," and who "are hypocrites" who "inside their hearts grind their teeth like a dog who... bites with its sharp teeth," and who "are like hens who make noise during the night and terrify themselves"?

Who is this woman who warns, "People who act like this aren't rooted in goodness"? They weren't then, and they aren't today.

Who is this woman who wrote to abbots telling them they were "grumbling like bears" and "in many ways bungling as well"?

Who is this woman who preached in monasteries and churches throughout Germany and Switzerland, denouncing corruption among the clergy and calling the church to repentance and to wake up?

Who is this woman who puts *justice* as the deciding ethical norm in ecclesial and cultural life, instead of blind obedience and christofascism?

Who is this woman who even wrote King Konrad III and told him to "get hold of himself" and put justice first?

Who is this woman who took on the Emporer Barbarosa, comparing him to an infant and a madman, and threatened that God's sword would smite him?

Who is this woman who painted pictures of church and society covered in human excrement because of patriarchal corruption?

Who is this woman who speaks of Christ and the "Word" as head of the church, not the pope and his curia?

Who is this woman who challenges a church today that has succumbed to advanced patriarchy and papalolatry, and is being run aground by a curia that is nothing more than a boys' club practicing power games and involved in a gross theological schism?

Who is this woman and Trojan horse whose theology of justice and compassion is in complete opposition to the right wing agenda of the last forty-two years of the papacy, which has supported dictators such as Pinochet and fascist movements like Opus Dei, Communion and Liberation, and Legion of Christ, while emasculating justice-oriented movements such as liberation theology and creation spirituality?

Who is this woman who compares her experiences to those of the apostles at Pentecost and paints a picture about it—and who compares her work of speaking the truth to people in power to that of the prophets Ezekiel and Daniel?

Who is this woman who dares to call herself a prophet, comparing herself to David who slew Goliath and Judith who slew Holofernes?

Who is this woman who insisted that not only she, but all Christians need to be "strong warriors" in taking on the demonic powers of one's time?

Who is this woman who speaks to women everywhere—and to all men who are brave enough to explore both the Divine Feminine *and* the Sacred Masculine in themselves and society?

◆

The facts of Hildegard's life are straightforward enough. She was born in 1098 at Bermersheim near Mainz, Germany, the youngest of ten children. Her parents, Mechthild and Hildeberts, were ranked in the lower free nobility. Around eight years of age, she was entrusted to the care of a holy woman named Jutta, daughter of the Count of Sponheim, who had connections to Hildegard's father. Together Jutta and Hildegard entered the Benedictine monastery of Disibodenburg on November 1, 1112, All Saints Day. Jutta became superior to a small community of women that developed at the monastery. Hildegard remained under Jutta's tutelage for thirty years. When Jutta died in 1136, Hildegard became the magistra, or teacher and leader at the age of 38.

Hildegard and her sisters left Disibodenberg to found a monastery called Rupertsberg in 1150. Fifteen years later, Hildegard founded another monastery in Eibingen. Hildegard received three visions that urged her to write: one in 1141, the second in 1163, and the third in 1167. To "speak and write" what she heard and saw were the instructions that accompanied the first vision. The result was her first book, *Scivias*, ("Know the Ways"), which took her ten years to write and which includes many paintings and ends with an opera! Her second major work, *Liber vitae meritorum* ("Book of the Rewards of Life"), focuses on morality and psychology, vices, and virtues to overcome them. This book took her five years to write. Her third visionary book, *Liber divinorum operum* ("Book of Divine Works"), was undertaken over a seven-year period and was completed in 1174. In it she presents ten visions devoted to creation and salvation, including an exegesis of John 1 and the Book of Revelation.

Among Hildegard's other expositions were books on medicine such as *Causae et cure* ("Causes and cures") and *Physica* (which draws on elements of nature, including stones, trees, fish, and more, for cures to ailments), the lives of Saints Disibod and Rupert, commentaries on the Rule of Saint Benedict and the Athanasian Creed, and a Commentary on the gospels (*Expositiones evangeliorum*), along with over 300 letters. She also wrote a book in which she invented her own language.

At the age of eighty, Hildegard was interdicted by the archbishop for a full year, which is akin to excommunication for her and all her sisters—an interdiction that was lifted only six months before she died. The point of contention was that the archbishop wanted her to remove the body of a revolutionary young man who was buried on her property, and she refused. Ultimately she won the argument, and the body is still there to this day.[4]

In this book we will go much deeper than mere facts, to where Hildegard wants to take us: deep places in our own hearts and souls, the "cave of our hearts" as Bede Griffiths put it, the "house of wisdom" that Hildegard teaches dwells in us all. We intend to travel into meditation and contemplation, into places of union and communion that ultimately lead to *appreciation*.

As Rabbi Heschel teaches, humanity will be saved not by more information, but by more appreciation. It is gratitude and its sister praise that we seek. Not praise of Hildegard as such—though she deserves a ton of it—but praise for existence itself. Praise for our glorious Planet Earth, our Mother. Praise for our powers of co-creation and creativity that are capable of moving us from the stuck places we find ourselves in as a species—our stuck religions, stuck education, stuck economics, and stuck politics—to a place more worthy of our noble origin in "original wisdom." Praise that joins in with the praise from the whole of nature, "the blowing wind, the mild, moist air, the exquisite greening of trees and grasses—in their beginning, in their ending, they give God their praise."[5] This is the praise we want to participate in.

Is this possible? With Hildegard as a guide, anything seems possible. I have seen her do her magic on all kinds of people, young and old, male and female, believer and non-believer.

Hildegard tells us things about herself that are anything but thoughts of a scared and passive woman. At the end of her first book *Scivias*, she hears God say to her and about her, "I will confuse all of these with a little and very tiny one, just as I cast Goliath down with a boy, and as I conquered Holofernes with Judith. Whoever will have rejected the mystical words of this book, I will stretch my bow above that person, and I will pierce that person with the arrows of my quiver. I will cast the crown from his or her head, and I will make that person like those who fell at Horeb (Sinai), when they murmured against me. And whoever will bring forth evil sayings against this prophet, that curse which Isaac brought forth will come upon him or her. Let people be satisfied with the heavenly rose when they embrace it and when they hold it in their heart and when they lead it forth into the level ways (Isaiah 40:4 and Luke 3:5)."

Notice that Hildegard has here compared herself (a "very tiny one") to David who took on Goliath and defeated him, and to Judith who beheaded Holofernes. She names herself as an author of "mystical words," a "prophet," a heavenly rose.

Hildegard continues with warnings from divinity about the importance of receiving the message of her first book: "Whoever has tasted the mystical words of this book and placed them in his or her memory, let this person be like a mountain of myrrh and frankincense, and all the other aromas. Let this person ascend by means of many blessings from blessing to blessing, just as Abraham did... But if any person will conceal these words of the finger of God fearfully and will lessen them through his or her own madness, or will have led them forth into a strange place by reason of some other human sense, let this person be condemned. The finger of God will rub this one away."[6] God says through her: "Receive these sermons and place them in your inner hearts (Luke 9:44). Do not refuse to listen to this warning. For I am the living and true witness of truth, and the speaking and *not-being-silent God*."[7]

We too who drink in the words and images, the music and visions of Hildegard eight centuries after she composed and lived them, are invited to ascend by means of "many blessings from blessing to blessing, just as Abraham did." The works of the Spirit are far from finished. The words of God haven't all been spoken. God is a "not-being-silent" divinity. Not in Hildegard's day and not in our own is Spirit finished. The Spirit, by Hildegard's testimony, is alive and well, urging us to live before all else "not lukewarmly," but "with passion and with blood."

◆

"Receive these sermons and place them in your inner hearts. Do not refuse to listen to this warning. For I am the living and true witness of truth, and the speaking and *not-being-silent God.*"

◆

An amazing part of Hildegard's story is that we still have so much of her work thanks to her Benedictine sisters who kept all of it for 800 years, including her writings, paintings, correspondence, and music—an amazing treasure trove of brilliance. In the year 1944, when the American bombers were coming over Germany, her sisters packed it all up to preserve it, sending it to Dresden where it was sadly firebombed. But smartly, the sisters copied everything before sending it. So what we have today is a first-generation copy of all her materials.

While Hildegard's is an amazing story, one still has to ask: How many women through the ages didn't have a whole nunnery to preserve their works for 800 years through wars and famines? How much of women's wisdom has been lost to us over the centuries? What is so remarkable in Hildegard's case is that none of her wisdom has been lost.

Hildegard is a woman who found her voice. Her God is a

"not-being-silent God." Women the world over today are learning to find their voice, to be the prophets and truth tellers all adults are called to be. Hildegard leads from a silenced God to a God who speaks through a woman. The Divine Feminine is back!

Chapter 2

LIVING WORDS AND THE COSMIC CHRIST

Hildegard meets Mary Oliver

For Hildegard, words are alive, and words take many forms that carry us beyond what we think of when we hear the word "word." For Hildegard, word is music and music is word. A "resounding melody" is inherent in every being, and a resounding melody is found in every single corner of the universe. The whole universe is vibrating with music, making melody.[1]

Hildegard examines her experience of melody resounding everywhere and contrasts it to the teaching in John's Gospel of the "Word of God." She combines music and word. The Word of God is everywhere and in everything, for "without the Word of God no creature has being. God's Word is in all creation, visible and invisible."[2]

Hildegard is teaching about the Cosmic Christ, for the Cosmic Christ—or cosmic wisdom—is the image of God in all things. It's the light in everything, as science today assures us that there are light waves or photons in every atom in the universe. Hildegard often saw the light in all things. She painted it and set it to music, which is why she speaks of her paintings, visions, and mandalas as "illuminations." Light beings bear light and reveal by way of light.

Notice that for Hildegard the "Word of God is in all beings whether visible or invisible." So even the darkness contains the light, the Word of

God, the Cosmic Christ, which is cosmic wisdom. It's everywhere, and it renders all beings holy, all beings luminous and numinous, full of creativity and generativity. To have *being* is to be a temple for the Word of God.

What's the nature of this Word? "The Word is living, being, spirit, all verdant greening, all creativity."[3] At the heart of the Word, at the heart of all beings, is creativity and "all verdant greening." All things are fertile, all things busy birthing and creating. How contemporary is Hildegard's view of the world! We can't escape the ever evolving, ever creating, and ever passing nature of created things. This is postmodern science, since creativity is one of the patterns inherent in evolution. It's also Hildegard's awareness in the 12th century! We are all verdant, all green, all busy creating: "All creation is awakened, called, by the resounding melody, God's invocation of the Word."[4]

I'm fascinated by how often Hildegard uses the term "all." She's constantly looking at the *whole* of things, the *gestalt* of things, the *cosmos* (which means "whole" in Greek). This too makes Hildegard truly postmodern—for as physicist David Bohm puts it, "a postmodern physics begins with the whole." Whereas modern physics was more zeroed in on the part, postmodern physics has more in common with premodern thinking than with modern thinking. It puts the whole, the "all," first.

In Hildegard's view of things, "all creation" is active. It isn't passive—not just sitting there, not enduring in a mode of "couchpotatoitis." Quite the opposite. All creation is *awakened* and *called*. It boasts a calling, a vocation, a reason for being, an invitation to participate and make things happen. This is true of stones and rocks, of trees and animals, of birds and sun and moon. And it's surely true of humans. We are called to "co-create," to live out our awakening, our calling, our greening power, our creativity and verdancy.

For Hildegard, it's God or Spirit who does the awakening and the calling, for God is invoking the "Word" that "manifests in every creature." Yet true to Cosmic Christ consciousness, "the Word is indivisible from God." In other words, everything we have said about creatures—everything we observe about sun and moon, galaxies and stars, whales and

cats, rosebushes and redwood trees, mountains and rivers, you and me—
all this is a manifestation of the divine Word, the divine Logos, the divine
wisdom that's alive in everything. All of this is *incarnation at work*, the
marriage of flesh and spirit. Thus Hildegard announces that "this is how
the spirit is in the flesh—the Word is indivisible from God."[5] Word and God
are one. We and God are one. All things and God are one.

Contemporary American poet Mary Oliver speaks to this same
understanding of spirit and flesh in tandem when she writes:

> The spirit
> likes to dress up like this:
> ten fingers,
> ten toes,
>
> shoulders, and all the rest
> at night
> in the black branches,
> in the morning
>
> in the blue branches
> of the world.
> It could float, of course,
> but would rather
>
> plumb rough matter.
> Airy and shapeless thing,
> it needs
> the metaphor of the body,
>
> lime and appetite,
> the oceanic fluids;
> it needs the body's world,
> instinct

and imagination
  and the dark hug of time,
    sweetness
    and tangibility,

to be understood,
  to be more than pure light
    that burns
      where no one is --

so it enters us --
  in the morning
    shines from brute comfort
    like a stitch of lightning;

and at night
  lights up the deep and wondrous
    drownings of the body
      like a star.[6]

I sense that Hildegard and Mary Oliver are on the same page—incarnation, and the holiness of the flesh. There's no dualism, that bedrock of patriarchal excess.

We have in this teaching from Hildegard, about the oneness of matter with the divine, echoes of Buddhism, for to be "awakened" is at the heart of Buddhist practice. Indeed, as we've already seen, the word Buddha means the "awakened one." Buddhism in its essence is all about waking up. All authentic spirituality is about waking up. As Kabir, the 15th century Indian mystic, remarked, "You have slept for millions and millions of years—why not wake up this morning?"

How asleep are we? How numbed are we by bad news and good news, by an overload of information and disinformation, by distractions such as the thousands of commercials we are subject to weekly while watching television, listening to the radio, or searching the internet? How *deeply* is our soul awake?

In declaring that the Word is manifest in every creature and that the Word *is* God, Hildegard is also making clear that all creation is *sacred*. Here she echoes Native American teachings about the sacredness of all beings—the four-legged and the cloud people, the winged people and the tree people. She calls us to return to respect and reverence, so that we don't take anything for granted.

"The blowing wind, the mild, moist air, the exquisite greening of trees and grasses—in their beginning, in their ending, they give God their praise."

Hildegard is singing about *panentheism*—we in God, as well as God in us. She is singing of how God is in things, and things are in God. She is singing about how things are *more* than "things," but are words of God—expressions of the divine being. Meister Eckhart 150 years later would say, "Every creature is a word of God and a book about God." Yes, a book about God, a revelation, a Bible. Hildegard believed this and experienced it. She *lived* it.

Hildegard experiences *praise* emanating from all beings—praise to their Creator. She writes, "The blowing wind, the mild, moist air, the exquisite greening of trees and grasses—in their beginning, in their ending, they give God their praise."[7] Poet Mary Oliver, who calls herself a "poet of praise," speaks in similar language when she talks of how trees give off their happiness and birds exude their joy all around us. There's a lot of praise going on in the world, if we only listen for it. The praise is of the Creator.

Are Mary Oliver's and Hildegard's experiences our experience too? Can we sit still long enough to feel this reality and hear the praise creation sings? Are we busy praising or are we preoccupied with problem solving or wallowing in depression, self-pity, and wounds others have inflicted on us?

Do we choose to praise? Do we hear the other creatures praising? Hildegard hears praise all around her—even in the wind and air, trees and grasses. In their origin and their destiny, they are busy extending praise. Has our species lost sight of its need to praise? How are we doing? Are we perhaps the only ones *not* praising?

To praise, we have to pay attention, which means we must be awake. We have to be still enough inside to observe the beauty, the goodness, and the gladness that's praiseworthy and going on all around us.

Mary Oliver gives us three "lessons for living." They are: 1) pay attention, 2) be astonished, 3) share your astonishment. Hildegard advises us, "Glance at the sun. See the moon and the stars. Gaze at the beauty of earth's greenings. Now, think. What delight God gives to humankind with all these things. Who gives all these shining, wonderful gifts, if not God?"[8]

Shining and wonderful, luminous and fiery, and filled with *doxa*—the Greek word for "glory" or "radiance," used at special times in the Scriptures—are these gifts of sun, moon, stars, and green things that flourish on the earth. They evoke in us *delight*. Joy is attached! Pleasure is among us. Enchantment surrounds us. The moon speaks to us. The sun blesses us with warmth, nurture, and food (as plants and animals absorb or "eat" sunlight and thereby flourish via photosynthesis). Delight indeed! Tasty things come home to our intimate breakfast and dinner tables. Many shining, wonderful, delicious gifts. Pay attention, and by so doing learn to praise.

Hildegard celebrates the *glory*—the radiance, or living light—that's in all beings. "There is no creation that does not have a radiance," she says. "Be it greenness or seed, blossom or beauty—it could not be creation without it."[9] All creation contains radiance or "glory." All beauty contains the same. We are struck with beauty and radiance many times every day. Hildegard is echoing the prophet Isaiah's awareness that "all of creation contains the glory of God" (Is 6.3). She tastes and breathes this glory.

Wisdom speaks to Hildegard: "I, the fiery life of divine wisdom, I ignite the beauty of the plains, I sparkle the waters, I burn in the sun, and the moon, and the stars. With wisdom I order all rightly. Above all, I determine truth."[10] There's a fiery life to wisdom, one that ignites, sparkles, burns, and keeps things in order. Even truth itself is full of this radiance and fire. Hildegard is deeply sensitive to this "living light," which so often appears in her visions and speaks to her in the first person.

When Hildegard was seventy-seven years old, she wrote the following description of her experiences: "From my childhood days, when my limbs, nerves, and veins

◆

"There is no creation that does not have a radiance. Be it greenness or seed, blossom or beauty—it could not be creation without it."

◆

were not yet strong, the gift of this vision brought joy to my soul; and this has remained true up to this very time when I am a woman of more than 70 years... The light which I see is not bound by space. It is much, much more light-filled than a cloud that carries the sun in itself. There is nothing in it to recognize of height, length, or breadth. It was described to me as the 'shadow of the living light.' And just as the sun, the moon, and the stars are reflected in water, so writings, talks, powers, and certain actions of people are illuminated for me in this light....

"It is in this light that I sometimes see, though not often, another light that I call 'the living light.' When and how I see this, I cannot say. But as long as I see this 'living light' all sadness and anxiety are taken away from me. The result is that I feel like a simple young girl and not like an old lady...."[11]

Words like "radiance," "numinosity," "glory," and "doxa" are synonyms for the Cosmic Christ, the image of God present and shining in all beings. This is like the Buddha Nature, which is also said to be present in all things, heightening our sense of reverence and respect. This teaching is about recovering a sense of the sacredness of all things. The Cosmic Christ is the Logos, or Word, that we have seen dwells in all things not passively but actively, urging them on to their rich fecundity and generativity—to the implementation of their greening powers.

In our time, Mary Oliver has named the Cosmic Christ richly and powerfully in her poem called "At the River Clarion." She writes:

1.

I don't know who God is exactly.

But I'll tell you this.

I was sitting in the river named Clarion, on a

water splashed stone

And all afternoon I listened to the voices

of the river talking.

Whenever the water struck the stone it had

something to say,

and the water itself, and even the mosses trailing

under the water.

And slowly, very slowly, it became clear to me

what they were saying.

Said the river: I am part of holiness.

And I too, said the stone. And I too, whispered

the moss beneath the water.

I'd been to the river before, a few times.

Don't blame the river that nothing happened quickly.

You don't hear such voices in an hour or a day.

You don't hear them at all if selfhood has stuffed your ears.

And it's difficult to hear anything anyway, through

  all the traffic, and ambition.

2.

If God exists he isn't just butter and good luck.

He's also the tick that killed my wonderful dog Luke.

Said the river: imagine everything you can imagine, then

  keep on going.

Imagine how the lily (who may also be a part of God)

  would sing to you if it could sing, if

    you would pause to hear it.

And how are you so certain anyway that it doesn't sing?

If God exists, he isn't just churches and mathematics.

He's the forest, He's the desert.

He's the ice caps, that are dying.

He's the ghetto and the Museum of Fine Arts.

He's van Gogh and Allen Ginsburg and Robert

Motherwell.

He's the many desperate hands, cleaning and preparing

  their weapons.

He's every one of us, potentially.

The leaf of grass, the genius, the politician,

   the poet.

And if this is true, isn't it something very important?

Yes, it could be that I am a tiny piece of God, and

   each of you too, or at least

      of his intention and his hope.

Which is a delight beyond measure.

I don't know how you get to suspect such an idea.

   I only know that the river kept singing.

It wasn't a persuasion, it was all the river's own

   constant joy

which was better by far than a lecture, which was

   comfortable, exciting, unforgettable.

3.

Of course for each of us, there is the daily life.

Let us live it, gesture by gesture.

When we cut the ripe melon, should we not give it thanks?

And should we not thank the knife also?

We do not live in a simple world.

4.

There was someone I loved who grew old and ill.

One by one I watched the fires go out.

There was nothing I could do

except to remember

that we receive

then we give back.

5.

My dog Luke lies in a grave in the forest,

   she is given back.

But the river Clarion still flows

   from wherever it comes from

     to where it has been told to go.

I pray for the desperate earth.

I pray for the desperate world.

I do the little each person can do, it isn't much.

Sometimes the river murmurs, sometimes it raves.

6.

Along its shores were, may I say, very intense

cardinal flowers.

And trees, and birds that have wings to uphold them,

for heaven's sakes--

the lucky ones: they have such deep natures,

they are so happily obedient.

While I sit here in a house filled with books,

ideas, doubts, hesitations.

7.

And still, pressed deep into my mind, the river

keeps coming, touching me, passing by on its

long journey, its pale, infallible voice

singing.[12]

Yes, an understanding of the Cosmic Christ, or the Buddha Nature, *is* very important. Mary Oliver understands it profoundly, and she calls this understanding "a delight beyond measure." Hildegard also understood it, and she too was delighted beyond measure, touched by the ecstasy of it all.

Geologian Thomas Berry also considered the cosmological aware-ness to be of paramount significance today. He writes, "The small self of the individual reaches its completion in the Great Self of the universe... To move from this abiding spatial context of personal identity to a sense of identity with an emergent universe is a transition that has, even now, not been accomplished in any comprehensive manner by any of the world's spiritual traditions."[13] In Hildegard we have a cosmology that trumps psychology, as one also has in indigenous traditions. She's a leader in this movement, a herald of a "Great Self of the universe" awareness, one that's named by the Cosmic Christ consciousness. But in today's understanding, it's an emerging universe, a birthing universe—a temporal, not just spatial universe.

In humans, this same Word, Logos—the Cosmic Christ—renders us morally strong. As Hildegard sees it, it bears fruit in the practice of virtue. In her opera *Ordo Virtutum* (Order of the Virtues), she calls virtues "soldiers" and "sweet warriors" who do battle against the "deceiver." Virtues are *powers* for Hildegard, whether we are speaking of constancy or humility, justice or joy: "We virtues are in God and we remain in God, we are soldiers for the king of kings and we overcome evil by good... O king of kings, we are fighting in your battle."[14] We imitate the Word when we stand strong in virtue, since God tells Hildegard that "my Word is a very strong warrior."[15] We too are called to be warriors or prophets by the Word dwelling in us.

Hildegard speaks about the church as the body of Christ, but for her the head of the church is *not* the pope or bishops. On the contrary, "The head of the church (Ephesians 5:23) is the Word of God; the womb and the other members of the body is the church itself with its members." Thus the Cosmic Christ is the head of the church, and the church is evolving, still very much unfinished, a work in progress: "The church, however, has not been completed yet, but it will be at the end of the world."[16]

By saying that the Word is at the head of the church, Hildegard is urging believers not to look to hierarchical structure so much as to the role of the Word in one's own heart and mind—in the decisions we make and the virtues we choose to cultivate. The church is less a noun than it is a verb, which means that it's wherever justice and peace, harmony and constancy are practiced.

Indeed, Hildegard lashes out at the corruption in the church of her day and even proposes that her words are a kind of "new scripture" to be heeded because the inherited Scriptures are not being attended to: "Pay attention to this sermon, and do not be incredulous of it. For if you spurn this sermon, you not only despise that, but myself—your God—as well. And I *am speaking the truth* (John 3:33) to you."[17] Yes, God was talking through her writings—she had no doubt about that.

Hildegard believes that the gospel has "stood firm" through the "time of times" and has "been proclaimed openly in the whole world." But trouble is on the horizon because "the catholic faith now staggers in people, and the gospel limps. The very scrolls which the best teachers had explained zealously in detail dissolve with foul disgust. And the food of life found in the divine Scriptures is lukewarm. Therefore, I—as your God—speak now through this human person [Hildegard] rather than through the Scriptures. This human person has not been taught to say these things by an earthly master, but I who am, speak through her. I speak the new secrets and the many mysteries which had previously been concealed within the scrolls."[18]

The I-who-am speaks through Hildegard rather than through the Scriptures alone. Hildegard too is the Word of God. The Word is alive and well even if Scriptures have often fallen into disuse or overfamiliarity. Remember that in Hildegard's day the Scriptures weren't readily available to the public because there were no printing presses and all books had to be written by hand. Furthermore, only a small portion of the population was literate. People depended on the monasteries for the keeping of the Scriptures.

Hildegard is emphasizing that there are many expressions of the "Word of God" beyond written scriptures—just as Meister Eckhart would say 150 years later, when he stated that if he would spend enough time with a caterpillar, he would never have to prepare a sermon, since every caterpillar too is a "Word of God." Words are not mere human words, and certainly not words on a page. "Every creature is a Word of God and a book about God," says Eckhart—Hildegard included. Indeed, each of us included.

Chapter 3

THE GOD OF LIFE AND LIGHT OR THE GOD OF RELIGION?

Hildegard meets Howard Thurman

By making clear distinctions between Scripture and her experience of God, and by demarcating the "head" of the church as the Word—the Cosmic Christ rather than any ecclesial official—Hildegard is putting forward a theology that the great African American theologian and spiritual leader Howard Thurman espoused: a God of life who takes precedence over a God of religion.

Thurman was an American mystic and prophet who was the spiritual teacher behind Dr Martin Luther King, Jr and the civil rights movement. Raised in a segregated town in Florida, his grandmother—a former slave—had a lasting influence on him. In 1935, he and his wife traveled to India where, among other memorable encounters, they spent time with Gandhi, who urged him to bring nonviolent civil disobedience to America.

Thurman wrote ten powerful books on spirituality, including *Jesus and the Disinherited* in which he lays out his conviction that Jesus' teaching has often been "betrayed" by the church, for he sees the gospels as a means by which the oppressed or disinherited can learn while their backs are against the wall. Dr King is said to have carried that one book with him every time he went to jail, which was thirty-nine times.

When religion is healthy and doing its job well, the distinction between the God of life and the God of religion need not apply. But when religion demonstrates signs of losing its way, as in Hildegard's world of the 12th century and ours of the 21th century, the distinction Thurman and Hildegard make is crucial.

Says Thurman, "At long last it seems to me that the customary distinction between religion and life is a specious one... All life, indeed all experience, is heavy with meaning, with particular significance."[1] He continues, "God is not merely the Creator of all creatures, of all objects animate and inanimate; but also, and more importantly, God is the Creator of life itself. Existence is the creation of God; life is the creation of God. This is of more than passing significance."[2] Indeed it is! Hildegard felt the same way. "God is life," she says. "Who is the Holy Trinity? You are music, you are life."[3]

Thurman gets excited on more than one occasion at the *aliveness* of life: "We are so overwhelmed by the personal but vast impact of the particularity of living objects that we are scarcely aware of a much more profound fact in our midst and that is that life itself is alive."[4] He exclaims a second time, "Life is *alive* [sic]; this is its abiding quality as long as it prevails at all. The word 'life' is synonymous with vitality... We are so conscious of the fact of each individual expression of life about us that the simplest and most wonderful fact of all is passed by. And what is that? The fact that life itself is alive, has the persistent trait of living—that any and all living things continue to survive as long as that essential vitality is available to them."[5] Vitality is an excellent synonym for spirituality. To be spiritual is to be aware—and thus fully alive, truly vital.

Hildegard attributes this sacred aliveness directly to the Holy Spirit when she calls the Holy Spirit the "Life of the life of all creatures."[6] Furthermore,

> Holy Spirit is
> Life-giving-life,
> all movement.

Root of all being.
Purifier of all impurity.
Absolver of all faults.
Balm of all wounds.
Radiant life, worthy of all praise,
The Holy Spirit resurrects and awakens everything that is.[7]

For Hildegard, "God is life." Indeed, "God lives in every created thing."[8] Referring to the Negro spiritual *Deep River* from slave times, Thurman comments that "the goal and the source of the river are the same: the sea." So it is with life and God. "Life is like that! The goal of life is God! The source of life is God! That out of which life comes is that into which life goes. He out of whom life comes is He into whom life goes. God is the goal of man's life, the end of all his seeking, the meaning of all his striving. God is the guarantor of all his values, the ultimate meaning—the timeless frame of reference. That which sustains the flower of the field, the circling series of stars in the heavens, the structure of dependability in the world of nature everywhere, the stirring of the will of man to action, the dream of humanity, developed and free, for which myriad men, sometimes in solitariness in lonely places or in great throngs milling in crowded squares—all this and infinitely more in richness and variety and value is God."[9]

Hildegard is equally ecstatic in naming the God of life and light when she writes:

Invisible life that sustains ALL,
I awaken to life everything
in every waft of air.
The air is life,
greening and blossoming.
The waters flow with life.
The sun is lit with life.
The moon, when waning, is again rekindled by the sun, waxing
    with life once more.

The stars shine,
Radiating with life-light.
All creation is gifted with the ecstasy of God's light.[10]

Life and light are companions. Thurman draws his ethics and morality from this reality when he says that "to deal with men on any other basis, to treat them as if there were not vibrant and vital in each one the very life of the very God, is the great blasphemy."[11]

Thurman saw life as "essentially dynamic and alive," an "essential process" that by its nature discounts the philosophy of the oppressor who wishes for a universe that's permanent and unchanging and "stacked" against the poor and oppressed. Hope arises when people can see that the contradictions of life aren't ultimate and that humanity isn't "caught in the agonizing grip of inevitables," After all, life isn't in essence "fixed, finished, unchanging."[12] God is active. Spirit is active. Indeed, as the Negro spiritual puts it, "God's gonna trouble the water" so that new life and freedom might arise.

Says Thurman, "This is the great disclosure: that there is at the heart of life a Heart. When such an insight is possessed by the human spirit, and possesses the human spirit, a vast and awe-inspiring tranquility irradiates the life." And here lies, in Thurman's view, "the most daring and revolutionary concept known to man: namely, that God is not only the creative mind and spirit at the core of the universe but that He...is love." This knowledge comes not by a "rational reflec-tive process," but by revelation or "disclosure."[13] All this gives hope to the downtrodden.

Hildegard agrees fully. At the heart of the universe is a heart: "Who is the Trinity? You are music. You are life. Source of everything, creator of everything, angelic hosts sing your praise... You are alive in everything, and yet you are unknown to us."[14] And the Word, so intimately present to all creatures, is life itself. The Word "reveals himself as the God of all creation and as the Life of life... No tongue would suffice to designate those who invoke God as the Life of all life. Blessed, therefore, are those who abide in God!"[15] The Word "appeared in every creature, and this sound was life in every creature."[16] Word and life are married for Hildegard, and both take precedence over institutional religion. After all, it's from such a creative word that religion gets renewed.

"Only the mystics bring what is creative to religion itself," observes psychologist Carl Jung. Mystics like Hildegard, Thurman, and Oliver break open the stale doors of institutional religion and God-talk to let the God of life speak anew. This is the meaning of Pentecost, the meaning of fire and Spirit descending once again.

Hildegard asks why the Word is called "Word" and answers that it "has awakened all creation by the resonance of God's voice and because he has called creation to himself!" In talking about life, we are talking about God; and in talking about God, we are talking about life, since "God is life to the fullest,"[17] and "it is God who can give life to deeds because God is life without any beginning whatsoever... God is the only life that does not originate in another form of life with a beginning."[18] The same Word that awakened all creatures also awakens us, and "the life that awakened the creatures is also the life of our own life, which becomes alive as a result."[19]

◆

"God is life to the fullest [and] God lives in every created thing."

◆

For Hildegard, God is also light, a "true light that gives light to all lights," and God "lives in every created thing." It's all the Cosmic Christ at work. The Word is "the Light of all lights, and it gives light of itself."[20] As I demonstrated in my book *One River, Many Wells: Wisdom Springing from Global Faiths*, light is the most universal of the metaphors ascribed to divinity among all the world's spiritual traditions. Thus Hildegard is very much in an ecumenical place with her emphasis on divinity and light. Hence she states, "We are flooded with light itself in the same way as the light of day illuminates the world."[21] God, she says, is the one "from whom all light is enkindled." Christ is "the true Light that gives light to all lights." The Cosmic Christ, or Word, is "the Light of all lights, and it gives light of itself."[22]

Hildegard refers to an ancient Jewish teaching about the "sparks of the *soul*"[23]—a teaching, by the way, that Howard Thurman thanks Meister Eckhart for and incorporates at the heart of his own teaching when he says that "what Eckhart calls the 'uncreated element' in [a person's] soul...was an assumed fact profoundly at work in the life and thought of the early slaves. This much was certainly clear to them—the soul of man was immortal. It could go to heaven or hell, but it could not *die*."[24]

Hildegard's connection of life, light, and word is a deeply Celtic conviction and reveals something of the rich Celtic influence she received. The Celts were acutely aware of their dependence on the sun, living as they were in a land of long, dark winters that rendered them appreciative of any and all signs of light—and with it life. Celtic scholar John O'Donohue informs us that among all the gods of ancient Ireland, Lugh, the god of light and giftedness, was the most venerated. "The Celtic mind adored the light," he explains. "Ultimately, light is the mother of life. Where there is no light, there can be no life... Light is the secret presence of the divine. It keeps life awake."[25]

Hildegard's words echo Celtic thinking when she declares, "I who am without origin and from whom every beginning goes forth, I who am the Ancient of Days, do declare that I am the day by myself alone. I am the day that does not shine by the sun; rather by me the sun is ignited. I am the Reason that is not made perceptible by anyone else; rather, I am the One by whom every reasonable being draws breath."[26] She honors the sun: "The sun is brightly shining; its light flashes; and the fire in it burns. It illuminates the whole world and appears as a unity. Everything in which there is no kind of power is dead, just as a branch cut off from a tree is dry because it has no greening power."[27]

The great ritual monument in ancient New Grange, Ireland, older than the Egyptian pyramids, was built around that one special day of light in the winter season—the winter solstice, the darkest day of the year in the northern hemisphere. The monument captures light on that one special day and carries it down a shaft into a chamber at the center of the ritual space.

Hildegard is also echoing Celtic wisdom when she stresses how words *live*. Words are alive. They carry Spirit. This teaching is

expressed eloquently in the many sculptors of the Green Man that graced the cathedral movement of Hildegard's time. The Green Man is often depicted with boughs and branches emerging from his mouth and throat, the location of the fifth chakra. Hildegard is celebrating this same truth when she speaks of the sacredness of the word. When we give birth to ideas, or to language and communication, we too are birthing from that birth canal that is our throat, our fifth chakra. Hildegard was fully cognizant of the Green Man movement of her time. As noted earlier, she even calls Christ "a green man" who caused "all the greening power of the virtues."[28]

Hildegard doesn't just wax eloquent about the divine light. She also sees humans as carriers of that light, as co-creators of light. For the Celts, light symbolized the intellect: "In the Celtic tradition, thought has often been compared to light. In its numinosity, the intellect was deemed to be the place of the divine within us."[29]

As well as praising our intellect as "our greatest treasure," Hildegard talks about the "living spark of the soul" that's inherent in every human. We are, she teaches, attractive to other creatures because we embody this light: "These creatures often rush toward us humans and attach themselves to us with great affection." Light and love bind us to other creatures: "We, too, have a natural longing for other creatures and we feel a glow of love for them."[30] Love glows and shines from humans to other creatures.

Chapter 4

HILDEGARD AS ECO-WARRIOR

Loving and Defending Mother Earth

It stands to reason that a theology that celebrates the Cosmic Christ or Buddha Nature of every forest and whale, every field and river, every stone and tree, is going to be eager to defend such sacred beings. Hildegard is that way. She defends Mother Earth and all her creatures unabashedly—and she urges us to do the same. Her disgust at "dryness" and not caring is palpable.

The way Hildegard cuts through denial is out front and upfront. Indeed, she expects all of us to be prophets and warriors on behalf of Mother Earth. "O human," she shouts, "why do you live without passion, without blood?" We're not here just to slip by—and certainly not to take for granted what nature gifts us with. To defend Mother Nature is to defend the Cosmic Christ.

This is why Hildegard teaches that injustice is dry, whereas justice is wet: "When you lack the verdancy of justice, your soul is dry, totally without tender goodness, totally without illuminating virtue." A dry person, a passionless and uncaring person, a person in denial, is "totally lacking" in virtue and "totally without goodness."[1]

For Hildegard, the earth and the universe are all one being coming to life. They aren't neutral or ho-hum, but glorious, radiant, filled with the brilliance of the Cosmic Christ. Hence she comments, "God has made heaven and earth in great glory." We have already seen how rich a term "glory" is to her. It's a code name for the Cosmic Christ.

Geologian and eco-prophet Thomas Berry talks of how "ecology is functional cosmology," and as we get to know Hildegard, we learn that she is as interested in the earth as in the universe—as ecological as she is cosmological. She tells us that "the earth is at the same time Mother. She is the Mother of all that is natural, Mother of all that is human. She is the Mother of all, for contained in her are the seeds of all."[2] This ancient teaching, found among indigenous peoples in the Americas—and also in Africa and many other lands, as well as in certain scientific circles—is the understanding of earth as Gaia, a single, interconnected eco system—or better, a network of eco systems.

The first time I taught Hildegard, I read the following "I am" poem by her to the class:

I am the one whose praise echoes on high.
I adorn all the earth.
I am the breeze that nurtures all things green.
I encourage blossoms to flourish with ripening fruits.
I am led by the spirit to feed the purest streams.
I am the rain coming from the dew
That causes the grasses to laugh with the joy of life.
I call forth tears, the aroma of holy work.
I am the yearning for good.[3]

On hearing the poem, a student spoke up: "I have been living on an Indian reservation in South Dakota for the last sixteen years. That woman you just cited sounded exactly like my spiritual director, who was a medicine man on the reservation." Yes, Hildegard's deep premodern consciousness—her awareness of the life going on all around us in and through the grasses, the blossoms, the fruits, the streams and rains and dew—all this celebration of the fertility of creation is ancient wisdom and ancient awareness. It's something we're in danger of losing as more and more of us live in cities cut off from the land, the seasons, the trees and plants, the birds and animals.

We place our souls in jeopardy to the extent we live apart from the richness of the rest of creation. Without this richness, our lives are less than alive. Our worlds are dangerously close to being circumscribed by technologies such as television and all things anthropocentric. We suffer from "nature deficit disorder," which is why we feel lost and cosmically lonely, often without having words for our condition, just an emptiness in our soul and boredom in our psyche. We feel we have little or nothing to praise, little or nothing to be thankful for. Hence we don't feel at all at home with Hildegard's praise consciousness when she writes, "Be not lax in celebrating. Be not lazy in the festive service of God. Be ablaze with enthusiasm. Let us be an alive, burning offering before the altar of God!"[4]

So anthropocentric has religion become—just like education, economics, and politics—that when we hear the word "religion," we usually think of such things as church buildings, church officials, dogma, canon law, clergy, vestments, and seminaries—not to mention non-profit status and tax deductions. None of this constitutes the essence of religion.

Thomas Aquinas, who lived fifty years after Hildegard, says that religion is, at its base, a *virtue*—a virtue of gratitude, a way of saying "thank you." This presumes that religion is essentially about praise, and therefore fundamentally an inner thing—a soul thing, not a building or institutional thing.

Virtues reside in us as habits. But it requires time and attention, a spirit of meditation and stillness and receptivity, to build up a sense of gratitude and praise. It requires paying attention. Hildegard knew this well, which is one reason she attacks church corruption, along with lazy clergy and church leaders, with such vehemence. They are abandoning their vocations, leaving the people with so little to feed the soul.

Consider how in America today, though we constitute 4% of the world's population, we use over 64% of the world's illicit drugs. Our news broadcasts report the horrible goings on in Mexico among drug gangs, with over 50,000 killed in drug wars there in the past few years.

But how truthful is our media about the *cause* of the immense business that the drug trade represents? Does the media report this to us, or just the symptoms?

The cause of the drug killings lies not so much in Mexico as in the United States, where it's obvious that something is missing in peoples' lives. There's a great emptiness of soul in America that yearns to be filled, and people feel that drugs are the answer. The drug *supply* may be in Mexico, but the *demand* arises from empty-souled North Americans. All the promises of the gods of consumer capitalism have in no way satisfied the yearning of the heart. Therein lies the core of the drug problem and the drug killings. Without the demand for drugs from empty-souled North Americans, the drug trade would dry up overnight. Something is amiss in the American soul.

One reason a feeling of emptiness prevails is that religion is so without energy, without power. Religion is "insipid," as Rabbi Abraham Heschel puts it. The fundamentalist and anti-intellectual wing of Christianity—including the current Vatican—blames it on secular science. But Heshel addresses the real cause.

Heschel writes, "It is customary to blame secular science and anti-religious philosophy for the eclipse of religion in modern society. It would be more honest to blame religion for its own defeats. Religion declined not because it was refuted, but because it became irrelevant, dull, oppressive, insipid. When faith is completely replaced by creed, worship by discipline, love by habit; when the crisis of today is ignored because of the splendor of the past; when faith becomes an heirloom rather than a living fountain; when religion speaks only in the name of authority rather than with the voice of compassion—its message becomes meaningless."[5]

Heschel isn't alone among religious leaders who dare to criticize religion itself. Howard Thurman said that Christianity "betrayed Jesus." Teilhard de Chardin, Jesuit priest and mystic, poet and scientist, said that "our religion is becoming enfeebled." Why? "Because it is not sufficiently moved by a truly human compassion, because it is not exalted by a sufficiently passionate admiration of the universe, our religion is becoming enfeebled." He wrote these words over sixty years ago.

Is religion becoming enfeebled? Has it deteriorated since Teilhard's time? Well, ask yourself, have we grown in a deeper compassion? Have we grown in a more passionate admiration of the universe?

Dietrich Bonhoeffer, a German Lutheran pastor who stood up to Hitler and paid the ultimate price, wrote from his prison cell before he was executed, "God calls us not to a new religion but to life." He also stated, "Christianity stands or falls with its revolutionary protest against violence, arbitrariness, and pride of power and with its pleas for the weak. Christians are doing too little to make these points clear rather than too much. Christendom adjusts itself far too easily to the worship of power. Christians should give more offense, shock the world far more than they are doing now. Christians should take a stronger stand in favor of the weak rather than considering first the possible right of the strong."[6]

The late scientist Gregory Bateson also opined about religion's failures when he asked whether humanity is "rotting its mind from a slowly deteriorating religion and education."

Thomas Berry believed that the "greatest failures of the twentieth century were religion and education." Both contribute to the "autism" (Berry's word), the pathological anthropocentrism that has us destroying the earth, killing our Mother, boring our souls, investing in violence, putting knowledge ahead of wisdom and patriarchy ahead of a sacred and balanced marriage of masculine and feminine, yin and yang.

Hildegard doesn't lack either a sense of truly human compassion or a passionate admiration of the universe, as we have seen. She doesn't lack a feminine perspective on divinity. Indeed, she declares that "God hugs you. You are encircled by the arms of the mystery of God."[7] Her mind and imagination were in no way rotting away and in no way autistic. She took on emperors and abbots, popes and politicians, who preferred pride of power to "lady justice." She understood education to be about cultivating wisdom—and this by way of cultivating creativity—and never saw it as developing knowledge for power's sake. Like Bonhoeffer and

Thurman, she prefers life to religion if it comes down to a choice. Hers is a God of life far more than a God of religion.

Years ago I shared the podium at the annual E.F. Schumacher Society in Bristol, England, with Lester Brown of the Worldwatch Institute. His talk preceded mine, and in it he called for an "environmental revolution," warning that the number one obstacle to this revolution would be human "inertia." Inertia, or "lukewarmness," is something Hildegard often writes about. We've seen that her most common criticism of the clergy is that they lack passion and are lukewarm. Inertia is best understood in the rich medieval language as *acedia*, one of the deadly capital sins that we often translate as "sloth," but which means much more, including sadness, depression, boredom, cynicism, "couchpotatoitis," and passivity.

> "Creation is allowed in intimate love to speak to the Creator as if to a lover."

Aquinas defined this syndrome as "the lack of energy to begin new things." He also names the medicine. Zeal, he says—which is the opposite of *acedia*—"comes from an intense experience of the beauty of things." This means we defend the earth because we love her deeply, which involves recognizing and not taking for granted her brilliant and glorious gifts. With this deep love comes caring—and when you care, you work to defend what you cherish.

Hildegard was nothing if not in love with the earth. You can feel it in her words, in her images, in her ecstatic sense of delight with all things earthly. "Holy persons draw to themselves all that is earthy," she declares. So earthiness and love of the earth are part of holiness, just as Mary Oliver observed.

Says Hildegard, "As the Creator loves his creation, so creation loves the creator." Thus there exists a love affair between Creator and creation: "The creation, of course, was fashioned to be adorned, to be showered, to be gifted with the love of the Creator. The entire world has been embraced by this kiss."[8]

Intimacy between creation and Creator is felt throughout the world. We are in the midst of it. As Hildegard puts it, "Creation is allowed in intimate love to speak to the Creator as if to a lover."[9] Her creation story more resembles the Song of Songs in the Hebrew Scriptures than Genesis—and she is correct in saying that the Song of Songs *is* another creation story. Creator and creation are lovers; God and nature are lovers.

This is fundamentally different from Newton's idea that God is behind the sky, distant and apart. As Thomas Berry points out, it's also different from Benedict's image of God in an agrarian relationship with the earth, or even St Francis with his model of the universal community of creatures. There's an erotic dynamic to Hildegard's model of God and creation. As she explains, "God has gifted creation with everything that is necessary... Limitless love, from the depths to the stars, flooding all. It is the royal kiss of peace."[10]

Thomas Berry comments that Hildegard offers a whole new model by which to relate to the earth, which she recognizes "as a region of delight. We might almost say 'pagan' delight since she has overcome the undesirable aspects of pagan naturalism not from without but from within the experience. She has reached far into the emotionally exciting aspects of nature in a unique mode of Christian communion. She sees the creation-maker in the ancient manner of the fertility cults, a view she expresses in her statement that creation and Creator are related as a woman and a man. Only thus is the earth fruitful."[11]

Let's hear this in Hildegard's own words: "I compare the great love of Creator and creation to the same love and fidelity with which God binds woman and man together. This is so that together they might be creatively fruitful." It's because of this "erotic" bond," says Berry, that "the earth becomes luxuriant in its every aspect."[12] It took Hildegard to introduce authentic eros into the equation of eco-justice. "Erotic justice" I call it in my book *Original Blessing*.

We all have special relationships with nature. Where would we be without sun, moon, and stars? Without fish and whales, four legged beasts and winged birds? The answer is obvious: we wouldn't exist. The reality is that *interdependence* reigns. In fact, Hildegard says that of all the species on the planet, humans are the *most* dependent on the other species. We need the vast array of species more than they need us.

Do we praise the apple? Do we praise the peach? Do we praise the animals and birds, the trees and the flowers, the fish and the rocks? Do we praise the sun, rain, soil, and seasons? (Isn't one way of praising to leave things healthy and beautiful for future generations?) Do we praise the humans who harvest the crops? Do we praise the supernova that birthed the elements we eat—indeed, the elements we are made of? Do we praise the fireball that birthed the cosmos? Or does anthropocentrism only praise itself—only worship a narcissistic, self-congratulatory species, while taking 13.7 billion years of creativity for granted? How are we doing?

Hildegard didn't think our species was doing particularly well even in her day, the 12th century. Imagine if she were among us today reading about the disappearance of species at rates greater than any time in the last 65 million years. Imagine if she read the UN report of a year ago that if we continue on the path we are currently on, there will be no more fish in the ocean forty years from now. (The report also said that there is time, though not much, to turn things around—an effort that must begin with banning the giant fishing vessels that many governments subsidize.) Imagine if Hildegard saw the disappearance of soil and rainforests, or if she witnessed the climate change that's pursuing us. What would she say? What would she do, and demand that we do?

Even in the 12th century she was sounding the alarm. For instance, in one apocalyptic vision she says, "I looked again and behold, all the elements and all the creatures were shaking with horrible motion. The fire, the air, and the water broke open and moved the land. Flashes of lightning and claps of thunder clashed. Mountains and forests fell. As a result, all mortal things breathed forth their life... And I heard a voice speak with a voice so loud that it could be heard throughout the whole circle of the lands. It said: 'O you people who lie on the ground, rise up.'"[13] Once again Hildegard calls us to rise up, to wake up, to get up and get to work.

Recently I read a definition of hope from David Orr, an eco-philosopher Hildegard would appreciate: "Hope is a verb with the sleeves rolled up." Indeed, it's time to go to work to defend Mother Earth—to become the eco-warriors Gaia needs in order to survive.

If God is life as Hildegard teaches, then what's the killing of species and the radical maiming of life on the planet? Is it *deicide*? Is it the crucifixion of the Cosmic Christ all over again? If Christ is the divine light and image in all beings, then to destroy forests and fowl, oceans and fish, four legged ones and ozone, soil and waters, is to crucify the Christ. To kill things is to deprive them of greening power, which is to lay a pall of death over the planet.

Hildegard reports another vision: "The greening power of the virtues faded away, and all justice entered upon a period of decline. As a result, the greening power of life on earth was reduced in every seed because the upper region of the air was altered in a way contrary to its first destiny. Summer now became subject to a contradictory chill, while winter often experienced paradoxical warmth. There occurred on earth times of drought and dampness..."[14] Her words feel eerily appropriate for the climate change and global warming we are experiencing today.

Hildegard addresses the issue directly when she says, "Now in the people who were meant to green"—she is using "green" as a verb now, and says it's our task to green things—"there is no more life of any kind, there is only shriveled barrenness. The winds are burdened by the utterly awful stink of evil, selfish goings-on. Thunderstorms menace, the air belches out the filthy uncleanliness of the peoples. There pours forth an unnatural loathsome darkness that withers the green, wizens the fruit that was to serve as food for the people. Sometimes this layer of air is full of fog, which is the source of any destructive and barren creatures that destroy and damage the earth, rendering it incapable of sustaining humanity... God desires that all the world be pure in his sight. The earth should not be injured, the earth should not be destroyed."[15] Prophetic words, these—as applicasable as any to today's situation vis-a-vis the pain and suffering of Mother Earth and all her creatures.

Time and again Hildegard talks about the "web of creation," of which we are an integral part. A web has give and take to it; it isn't rigid but bends with the breeze. But injustice creates a rupture in the web, and Hildegard warns that "as often as the elements of the world are violated by ill treatment, so God will cleanse them through the sufferings, through the hardships of humankind."[16] Such hardships today include the great migrations of people who are leaving their homelands because of drought or rising seas. I've met people from the Pacific islands who tell me they need to pack up and leave because, as a result of global warming, the waters are inundating their freshwater tables, which means they can no longer grow crops. Thus they must abandon their islands.

◆

"As often as the elements of the world are violated by ill treatment, so God will cleanse them through the sufferings, through the hardships of humankind."

◆

These islanders are the canaries in the mines—warning signals of what may be coming to all of Florida, southern California, Manhattan, and many places around the world if we don't alter our lifestyle and thereby curb global warming.

How deeply in love we are—not with the beauty and health of the earth and future generations who deserve the same experiences we have had, but with our own denial. We hide behind it. Much of the political system of America bathes in denial of global warming and of the science that's trying to wake us up.

Hildegard warns, "The high, the low, all of creation God gives to humankind to use. But if this privilege is misused, God's justice permits creation to punish humanity."[17] It isn't a thunderbolt from on high that will punish humanity, but the failing web of life. Creation itself will seek its balance, thereby wreaking vengeance on our species. As Hildegard observed, we "are more dependent on the rest of creation than any other species... We are the guardian of creation."[18] Or at least, we ought to be.

Hildegard's passion for defending Mother Earth is palpable. One can only imagine the ways in which she would be busy waking people up were she here today, enlisting them in the development of alternative energy.

Hildegard's call to spiritual warriorhood on behalf of Mother Earth—her prophetic outrage and anger—parallels some of the preaching of Howard Thurman, who back in the 1950s, before Rachel Carson wrote her groundbreaking book *The Silent Spring* which launched environmental consciousness, offered a prophetic critique of our distorted relationship with nature. He writes about the spiritual loss that's felt when nature is left out: "Man cannot long separate himself from nature without withering as a cut rose in a vase. One of the deceptive aspects of mind in man is to give him the illusion of being distinct from and over against but not a part of nature. It is but a single leap thus to regard nature as being so completely other than himself that he may exploit it, plunder it, and rape it with impunity."[19]

This is why regaining Hildegard's perspective on our erotic bond with nature, and the divine's erotic bond with nature, is so healing and so needed. Eros is the opposite of denial. Eros isn't cold, indifferent, lazy, apathetic, or uncaring. Eros awakens. Hildegard put it this way: "The mysterious gifts of the Holy Spirit touch us human beings, who have begun to become dull as a result of our boredom. As a result, we shall awaken from our dullness and arise vigorously toward justice."[20] Eco-justice flows from waking up.

Thurman offered an additional warning about humanity's unhealthy relationship with nature and the sickness it breeds: "This we see all around us in the modern world. Our atmosphere is polluted, our streams are poisoned, our hills are denuded, wild life is increasingly exterminated, while more and more man becomes an alien on the earth and fouler of his own nest. The price that is being exacted for this is a deep sense of isolation, of being rootless and a vagabond. Often I have surmised that this condition is more responsible for what seems to be the phenomenal increase in mental and emotional disturbances in modern life than the pressures—economic, social and political—that abound on every hand. The collective psyche shrieks with the agony that it feels as a part of the death cry of a pillaged nature."[21]

Agony, death cry, shrieking—all of this speaks to the reality of our time, a reality that Hildegard foresaw and warned us about. Is this any way to treat our Mother? Hildegard would shout, "No!" There's no substitute for becoming Green Men and Women, for standing up and defending Mother Earth. It will take fortitude and spiritual warriorship to do so. It will take mystics (lovers) who are also prophets (warriors). Are we up to the task? Don't future generations beg us to "rise up"?

Chapter 5

HILDEGARD AND 21st CENTURY SCIENCE

Hildegard Meets Einstein

Recently I co-led an evening in the Episcopal Gothic Grace Cathedral in San Francisco with cosmologist Brian Swimme and organist Maryliz Smith. The theme of the evening, which was intended to be a contemplative event, was "Hildegard of Bingen Meets the New Cosmology."

Swimme had recently released his film *The Journey of the Universe*, which has played on over 325 PBS stations around the United States and recently won an Emmy. Including fundraising and filming, the creative project had absorbed much of his time and energy over a nine-year period—not an introverted scientist's primary love! Though he was exhausted from the experience, it was he who proposed the evening at the cathedral. Because he finds much in Hildegard that recharges the soul, he told me that even the idea of such a contemplative event imparted renewed life and energy.

One motivation for the occasion was to mark the 30th anniversary of his and my first meeting with Dr Thomas Berry—the "geologian," now deceased, with whom Swimme has written a major work entitled *The Universe Story,* and who was an invaluable mentor to Swimme and many others, myself included. It was at my Institute of Culture and Creation Spirituality at Mundelein College in Chicago that Swimme, Berry, and I first met up. As Swimme remembered, the day I met Berry, I launched into a discussion of Hildegard since I was writing my book of her illuminations. Immediately Berry responded in kind. He was the first living human being I had met who knew Hildegard.

I'm convinced that many scientists would enjoy knowing Hildegard, finding in her a valuable sister, just as Swimme and Berry have. Many of Hildegard's teachings are in tune with some of the most important findings of today's science. Let us consider some of these points.

1. A Cosmological Perspective and a Love of the Cosmos

We saw in chapter two what a pivotal role cosmology and the Cosmic Christ plays in Hildegard's worldview, and how physicist David Bohm talks about a knowledge of the "whole" that characterizes postmodern science. Hildegard was on a constant quest for a sense of the whole.

Because the whole and the cosmos furnished the entire *context* of her theology, how excited she would be to be studying the new cosmology! How pleased she would be to see faith-seekers moving from an overly *psychological* approach to religion, to a deeper and far more expansive *cosmological* approach. How thrilled she would be to discover the depth and wonder of the new cosmology, thanks to today's science.[1]

The 20th century saw an explosion of awareness of the universe. For Newton, the universe was only 50,000 years old and there was but a single galaxy. In his worldview, the universe was fixed and completed. How much we have learned since then about the unimaginable size, age, and continuing expansion of the universe! We inhabit a cosmos that contains at least 100 billion galaxies—some guess as many as 500 billion—and has been 13.7 billion years in the making. Our universe has been creative from the get-go. Beginning smaller than a zygote, it has expanded creatively all this time. Since all beings in the universe had their beginning in that original moment of flaring forth, all beings are kin. Today every school-child knows these amazing facts that Newton never knew.

Of course, Hildegard didn't know these facts either. However, she intuited some of them insofar as she, unlike Newton, didn't take a fixed, cold, mechanical clock as the model for her universe. Instead she paints the universe as an *egg*, and of course an egg is an incipient being that bespeaks beginnings, growth, and evolution. It also has a nest-like quality—so we might think of the universe as our nest, our home. Further, an egg is obviously a feminine image, since it gives birth to the life growing within it. An egg also holds great promise, in that it's the genesis of a new being and signals new beginnings. And an egg is organic, found everywhere in nature. Within an egg is a dynamic balance—a state of homeostasis, representing the justice that allows life to flourish. Also present is a passion for life. The elements of Hildegard's day—earth, air, fire, water—are integrated into her painting of the egg of the universe.[2]

Later in her life, Hildegard dictated three other cosmic visions of the universe as a sphere.[3] In her later life, scientists pictured the universe as a sphere, and she was clearly paying attention to them. Most important in Hildegard's depiction of the universe is the fact that she felt the cosmos was essential to an understanding of medicine, psychology, ethics, and religion. Unlike so many theologians of the modern era, so mired in anthropocentrism and cut off from cosmology and science, as mentioned earlier she casts her entire theology not in terms of *psychology* but in terms of *cosmology*. In her holistic view, we are citizens of the universe, not just of man-made institutions. Indeed, Hildegard's world-view encompasses the microcosm and the macrocosm. Today we understand as she did that our psyche is based on our relation to the universe and to all beings within it. Indeed, Carl Jung believed this holistic approach to be the psychology of the future.

Today's creation story begins with the "fireball" or "flaring forth" that occurred 13.7 billion years ago. Curiously, Hildegard writes and draws pictures of what she calls "fireballs" that enter the human baby when we are born. As she explains, "A fireball possesses the heart of this child... The fireball rules the entire body just as the firmament of heaven contains lowly things and covers celestial things and also touches the brain of the person. The fireball...pours itself through all the limbs of the person and gives the greenness of the heart and veins and all the organs to the entire body as a tree gives sap and greenness to all the branches from its root."[4] Today's science tells us the original fireball is present in our brain when photons light up with new ideas, and also in the process of photosynthesis, the greening of the plants. Thus when we eat plants, fish, or other creatures, we are ingesting "fireballs" that are descended from the original fireball.

2. About Light and a Cosmic Religious Feeling a la Einstein

As we also saw in chapter two, light plays a significant role in Hildegard's experience of Spirit, God, and life itself. Like Hildegard, Einstein was mesmerized by light and once said that all he wanted to do his whole life long was to study it.

In a remarkable book by a friend of Einstein in his days in Germany, who like Einstein emigrated to America, Einstein reveals more of his thinking about religion and spirituality. Sociologist and poet William Hermanns, in his book *Einstein and the Poet: In Search of the Cosmic Man*, relates an exchange Einstein had with a fundamentalist preacher who spent two hours trying to convert him to Jesus as his "lord and savior." It was during this encounter that Einstein articulated his view of healthy versus unhealthy religion.

Like Hildegard, Einstein connects science and the spiritual experience of awe, explaining, "There is no true science which does not emanate from the mysterious. Every thinking person must be filled with wonder and awe just by looking up at the stars."[5] It was this sense of awe and wonder that nourished Einstein from a young age, as he testified after being accused by the fundamentalist preacher of having "no respect for miracles."

Einstein's reply to this accusation is instructive: "You are mistaken. I have marveled often in my life. As a boy of twelve I already marveled at Euclid's geometry. Of course, what I thought was superhuman or miraculous was soon nothing but logical thinking added to experience. Still, I marvel every day, and it is my faith in the order of creation which makes me marvel. When I do so, however, I use logical thinking to find out why."[6] The ability to marvel coupled with the intellect is immensely important to Hildegard.

Hildegard marvels every day, which is why reading her work and hearing her music arouses wonder and awe, causing us to marvel. She also fully endorses our intellect or "left brain," for there's nothing anti-intellectual about Hildegard. As we saw earlier, she insists that "our greatest treasure is a living intellect," explaining that "all science comes from God." Like Einstein or any scientist, she holds study up for engagement. Indeed, study is a kind of prayer or meditation, for through it we learn to focus as we learn more about creation and therefore more about God and ourselves. Study can be a spiritual practice just as work is in the Benedictine tradition.

Hildegard calls Christ "Holy Rationality" and teaches that humans understand "all things" because we possess rationality.[7] Professor Kienzle recognizes that Hildegard identifies the "Word" or Logos as rationality: "She uses rationality here as the Son of God the *Logos,* but also as the rational faculty in the human being."[8]

When Hildegard teaches that the word is rationality and "God is rationality,"[9] she is saying that our employment of rationality is something "holy."[10] Indeed, rationality "leads the human being's five senses to God's righteousness."[11] We employ rationality when we study the scriptures.[12] Thus we can see that for Hildegard as for Einstein, awe and knowledge, mysticism and intellect, aren't at odds but are companions on the journey.

Einstein says, "In the face of creation I feel very humble. It is as if a spirit is manifest infinitely superior to man's spirit. Through my pursuit in science I have known cosmic religious feelings. But I don't care to be called a mystic."[13] Obviously Hildegard isn't shortchanged in the cosmic religious feeling department either. It leaps off the page in her writings, her music, and her poetry.

Einstein talks about mysticism when he says "there is a mystical drive in man to learn about his own existence... I believe that the dignity of man depends not on his membership in a church, but on his scrutinizing mind, his confidence in his intellect, his figuring things out for himself, and above all his respect for the laws of creation."[14] He also endorses the mystical when he stresses that "it is not intellect, but intuition which advances humanity. Intuition tells man his purpose in this life..."[15] He continues, "One never goes wrong following his feeling—I don't mean emotions, I mean feeling, for feeling and intuition are one."[16]

Hildegard would agree wholeheartedly. Feeling and intuition constitute the mystical dimension of our minds. They aren't at the expense of a "scrutinizing mind" or confidence in our intellect, however. Intuition and knowledge are in a dynamic dance, enjoying a dynamic relationship with each other.

3. Values and a Cosmic Religion a la Einstein

Einstein calls for a "cosmic religion" that will put conscience above allegiance to nationhood or religious institutions. "The most beautiful Church for me is the church of conscience, found in the silence of one's own presence," he proclaims. "A cosmic religion is the only solution— then there will be no more Church politics of supporting the mighty at the cost of the human rights of the poor."[17]

Einstein was reacting to the utter immorality of churchgoers in the Nazi era: "When I think of the tragic behavior of the German intellectual elite—famous scholars, ministers, and priests, generals [and many of them churchgoers, like Brauchitsch, Rundstedt, and Rommel!] I can only say that the welfare of humanity must take precedence over loyalty to one's own country or to one's church. I repeat, we need a cosmic religion."[18] A cosmic religion is post-tribal and post-anthropocentric.

Einstein resists rationalism and the idolatry of the intellect when he says, "Warn people not to make their intellect their god. The intellect knows methods but it seldom knows values, and they come from feeling." What are Einstein's prime values? "If one doesn't play a part in the creative whole, he is not worth being called human. He has betrayed his true purpose."[19] So our true purpose is to participate in the creative whole. As Einstein confesses, "I believe in one thing—that only a life lived for others is a life worth living."[20] Einstein and Hildegard are truly on the same page in this, for she talks about the two dimensions to being human, which are praise and the carrying out of good works: "It is in praise and service that the surprise of God is consummated."[21]

Einstein focuses on *vocation* when he talks about finding one's call or true purpose. Hildegard is living out hers and urges us to do the same. Speaking personally, Einstein says, "I have only one interest: to fulfill my purpose here where I am. This purpose is not given me by my parents or my surroundings. It is induced by some unknown factors. These factors make me a part of eternity. In this sense I am a mystic...those unknown factors mold our inner self."[22]

The minister I mentioned earlier asked Einstein whether he had faith in a life to come, to which Einstein replied, "No, I have faith in the universe, for it is rational. Law underlies each happening. And I have faith in my purpose here on earth. I have faith in my intuition, the language of conscience, but I have no faith in speculation about Heaven and Hell. I'm concerned with this time—here and now... We don't need to worry about what happens after this life, as long as we do our duty here—to love and to serve."[23] Hildegard would agree that intuition is the language of conscience, that a life lived for others is a worthy life, and that we are here to love and serve, for "God gave to humankind the talent to create with all the world...the good deeds shall glorify, the bad deeds shall shame."[24]

"One thing I know about my God," reported Einstein, is that "he makes me a humanitarian. I am a proud Jew because we gave the world the Bible and the story of Joseph. As long as I live, I will try to save lives."[25] Elaborating on his faith, he continued, "Judaism is not so much a creed as it is an ethical code that sanctifies life... I am concerned with this life... Shouldn't we do good for the sake of doing good, and not because we fear punishment or hope for reward in a life to come?"[26]

Einstein also provides us with insight into his understanding of the nature of God when he explains, "My religion is based on Moses: Love God and love your neighbor as yourself. And for me God is the First Cause. David and the prophets knew that there could be no love without justice or justice without love. I don't need any other religious trappings."[27] Hildegard would be on the same page with Einstein about love of God and neighbor, though her personal choice may be different when it comes to religious practices.

Einstein criticizes the bellicosity of America: "The atomic question is not so much a scientific as a moral one, you know. It disturbs me that, even though the atomic age is here, people still don't want to change their mode of thinking. Also, when I look around I see a new slavery for the individual developing in the United States. Everything seems to be in preparation for war rather than peace, glorifying the warlike spirit to cope with the Russian threat. This capitalist interest in armament production reminds me of the conspiracy of the Krupps and others with Hitler. War industry is a source of wealth. These industrialists owned castles, land, and yachts."[28] The situation has become worse since Einstein's day. Militarism rules, and fat paychecks for industrialists and profiteering Wall Street speculators have blossomed during the past ten years of wars in the Middle East, for example. Offshore tax havens abound.

In her day, Hildegard also criticized the bellicosity of humans and writes of apocalyptic visions she had in which "the course of time will hold up warlike people. They will wage many wars, but forget to think about the righteousness of God during those wars." But "these kingdoms will eventually begin to run into the weariness of feebleness" and a "son of destruction" will arise and deceive many. He is the antichrist, who "is the worst beast. He destroys people who deny him. He joins himself to kings, dukes, leaders, and wealthy ones. He presses down humility and lifts up pride. He subjects lands to himself with diabolical craft. His power goes forth right up to the edge of the wind so that he can stir up the air. He leads fire out of the sky with flashes of lightning, thunder, and hail. He throws down mountains. He dries up water... He never ceases deceiving people... So many will be deceived when they cover over their inner eyes. They should have looked at me (God) with their inner eyes."[29] The "inner eye" denotes consciousness, surely, as well as discernment and intuition.

If we look at the state of our world today, is not the war machine sapping the creative energy of nations? Are not people losing their jobs, their homes, and even going hungry, while billions are spent on wars that don't seem to resolve the issues at the root of the conflicts?

Hildegard personifies the unconsciousness of humanity by speaking of it as the "antichrist," as if it were a single individual—an image from the Book of Revelation. However, just as the Christ isn't a term restricted to the individual Jesus of Nazareth, but is divine consciousness seeking to come alive in all humans, so too the antichrist is the spirit of militarism, environmental destruction, and oppression that is rife in our world today.

Hildegard continues, "The son of destruction—the antichrist—works the deceits of his own crafts in the elements. He makes the beauty, sweetness, and pleasantness of the elements appear exactly according to the wishes of the person he is deceiving... Whatever the son of injustice works, he does it by power, pride, and cruelty—not with mercy, humility, and discretion. He uses majesty and astonishment to rush people along so that they will follow him... The antichrist shows people treasures and riches and allows them to feast according to their own wills."[30] The allurement of power and riches that accompany the warlike souls will prove hard to resist—just as Einstein predicted.

When Hildegard speaks of using "majesty and astonishment," I think of the arrogance of the expression "shock and awe," words that figured in the American administration's strategy at the time of the U.S. invasion of Iraq in retaliation over 9/11. The desire to impose our political and economic systems upon others—the impulse to have the whole world follow us in our ways—is, in Hildegard's view, an aspect of the spirit of antichrist.

4. The Importance of Science and Imagination

Einstein states that "science without religion is lame and religion without science is blind. They are interdependent and have a common goal—the search for truth. Hence it is absurd for religion to proscribe Galileo or Darwin or other scientists. And it is equally absurd when scientists say that there is no God... Without religion there is no charity. The soul given to each of us is moved by the same living spirit that moves the universe."[31]

Einstein insists that "imagination is more important than knowledge," something he knows from experience. It happens that his brilliant breakthrough with regard to the speed of light came essentially from an act of imagination when he was sixteen years old. He imagined what it would be like to ride on a photon—and from this his relativity theory was deduced! Hildegard too puts imagination and creativity out front, for it's the path to wisdom as distinct from mere factual knowledge. It constitutes the "greening" of our souls and of our work.

5. Interdependence

One of the lessons drawn from postmodern science is the ancient teaching of the interdependence of all things. This too represents a break with Newton and other modern thinkers who emphasized a kind of rugged individualism—a billiard ball theory of atoms, wherein only the independent survive. In contrast, today's insights are all about interdependence—how we're all connected, since all matter came into existence as a result of the original fireball.

Hildegard teaches interdependence as well. "God has arranged all things in the world in consideration of everything else," she declares.[32] There is an arrangement, a give and take, a system of interdependence everywhere we look, from oceans to forests, galaxies to black holes, planets to moons. Furthermore, Hildegard assigns this interdependence to the Holy Spirit at work within the interior of things when she says, "O

Holy Spirit, you are the mighty way in which every thing that is in the heavens, on the earth, and under the earth, is penetrated with connectedness, penetrated with relatedness."[33]

I want to draw your attention to the fact that not only is connectedness—relatedness—to be found everywhere, but it's found deep *within* things. All are "penetrated" with connectedness and relatedness, as Hildegard puts it. Such interconnectivity is within nature itself, manifest within every being in nature.

In other words, not the *ding-an-sich*—not substance—lies at the heart of reality, but relationship. This is feminist philosophy. It's also what Meister Eckhart taught 150 years later—the idea that "relation is the essence of everything that exists." It's what science is learning about the world of the microcosm and the macrocosm, which matches the teaching of indigenous people who honor "all our relations" when they pray.

> ◆
>
> "Holy Spirit, you are the mighty way in which every thing that is in the heavens, on the earth, and under the earth, is penetrated with connectedness, penetrated with relatedness."
>
> ◆

Physicist Fritjof Capra put it this way: "Subatomic particles have no meaning as isolated entities, but can only be understood as interconnections between the preparation of an experiment and the subsequent measurement. Quantum theory thus reveals a basic oneness of the universe. It shows that we cannot decompose the world into independently existing smallest units. As we penetrate into the matter, nature does not show us any isolated 'basic building blocks', but rather appears as a complicated web of relations between the various parts of the whole."[34]

Interdependence is also the bedrock of compassion. The Catholic monk Thomas Merton observed, "The whole idea of compassion is based on a keen awareness of the interdependence of all these living beings, which are all part of one another and all involved in one another." If compassion lies at the heart of both Einstein's ethic and Hildegard's, then here too we find common ground.

Hildegard talks frequently about the "web of creation," as does today's physics. Capra comments, "In the new world view, the universe is seen as a dynamic web of interrelated events. None of the properties of any part of this web is fundamental; they all follow from the properties of the other parts, and the overall consistency of their mutual interrelations determines the structure of the entire web."[35] Hildegard is surely on board with this further application of the principle of interconnectivity when she says, "Humanity finds itself in the midst of the world. In the midst of all other creatures humanity is the most significant and yet the most dependent upon the others."[36]

6. Consciousness

One of the most important questions in modern and contemporary science concerns consciousness. Where is it in the universe? Is it everywhere, as Buddhists teach? Is it in animals, plants, trees, and even rocks? Or is it only in humans?

◆

"no creature, whether visible or invisible, lacks a spiritual life."

◆

The much vaunted and influential physicist Stephen Hawking published a book on the universe in which he never mentions the word "consciousness." He does however come out of the closet as a scientific materialist. For scientific materialists, there's no "consciousness" anywhere.

Hildegard offers her answer to this pressing question concerning the presence of consciousness when she says, "It is written: 'The Spirit of the Lord fills the Earth.' This means that no creature, whether visible or invisible, lacks a spiritual life."[37] Thomas Berry speaks similarly when he says the universe is a community of *subjects*, not a collection of objects. Consciousness, an interior life, subjectivity—these are pressing topics in 21st century science.

No one knows this better than Rupert Sheldrake, the British biologist who in a new book entitled *The Science Delusion: Freeing the Spirit of Enquiry* takes on the scientific materialist's most sacred cows, daring to talk about the "dogmas" that remain unscientifically researched. The title of the book is a play on Richard Dawkins' book *The God Delusion*, Dawkins being one of the most vocal proponents of scientific materialism's efforts at atheism. Sheldrake presents a list of ten dogmas that constitute the "scientific creed" and proceeds to dismantle them chapter by interesting chapter. He is a scientist arguing that science itself needs to "be less dogmatic and more scientific," and that scientific thinkers need to be "liberated from the dogmas that constrict them."[38]

Sheldrake asserts that "science is being held back by centuries-old assumptions that have hardened into dogmas. The sciences would be better off without them: freer, more interesting, and more fun—and he is concerned that "the sciences have lost much of their vigor, vitality and curiosity" because fear-based conformity and dogmatic ideology in science is "inhibiting scientific creativity."[39] He calls his book "pro-science," and stresses that the beliefs of science "are powerful, not because most scientists think about them critically but because they don't." While the *facts* of science are real enough, the belief system behind scientific thinking amounts to "an act of faith, grounded in a nineteenth-century ideology."[40]

One of the dogmas Sheldrake addresses is that of the question of consciousness, which, he points out, is a profound question because the issue of a life beyond this one is pretty much determined by the answer one posits. He defines the scientific creed around this question: "All matter is unconscious. It has no inner life or subjectivity or point of view. Even human consciousness is an illusion produced by the material activities of brains."[41]

In raising this fundamental issue in the provocative way he does, Sheldrake is opening the door to Hildegard's direct answer to the question we are addressing, which is that no creature lacks an interior life. Annie Dillard also raised the question when she wrote a book called *Teaching a Stone To Talk*, and her answer was that they do talk, but it takes them 10,000 years to speak one word! However, if you've ever done a sweat lodge, you know from experience that some stones talk on the spot and don't have to wait 10,000 years. This is where spiritual practice enters and alters the equation.

Sheldrake observes that "the central doctrine of materialism is that matter is the only reality. Therefore consciousness ought not to exist. Materialism's problem is that consciousness does exist." The other scientific hypothesis known as dualism accepts consciousness but "has no convincing explanation for its interaction with the body and the brain."[42] Souls and God get eliminated in the scientific materialist view of consciousness. Some of the founders of that movement were militant atheists, whereas the dualistic tradition tended to keep a sense of God and soul by emphasizing the mind as immaterial and disembodied, and the body as a machine made up of unconscious matter.

Sheldrake points out that our legal and educational systems are based on a belief that we possess some degree of free choice and are responsible for our actions. "Even to discuss consciousness presupposes that we are conscious ourselves," he reasons. Nevertheless, the materialist belief-system "dominates institutional science and medicine, and everyone is influenced by it."[43]

Sheldrake puts forward what he calls a "third way," which is neither dualism nor rigid materialism. Panpsychism proposes that "even atoms and molecules have a primitive kind of mentality or experience." This doesn't mean that their consciousness is like ours, since more complex forms of mind or experience emerge from more complex systems. What seems to be the case is that "in *self-organizing* systems, complex forms of experience emerge spontaneously, more complex forms of experience emerge from less complex ones. There is a difference of degree but not of kind."[44]

The 17th century philosopher Baruch Spinoza, who was Einstein's favorite philosopher, wrote that "each thing, as far as it can by its own power, strives to persevere in its being... The striving by which each thing strives to persevere in its own being is nothing but the actual essence of the thing."[45] This is in line with Hildegard, who says that "no creature is without its own power." Meister Eckhart also celebrated how "each being is gladly doing its best to express God" and "all creatures may echo God in all their activities."[46] He observed that even a caterpillar, when it falls off a wall, strives to right itself in order to survive because "'isness' is so noble!" For Spinoza, the desire of a being to survive is an appetite and therefore an expression of consciousness.

Sheldrake raises the possibility that "all organisms, physical and biological, have experience and feelings, including atoms, molecules, crystals, cells, tissues organs, plants, animals, societies of organisms, ecosystems, planets, solar systems and galaxies." The matter is important, he insists, since we can think of ourselves "as a zombie-like mechanism" or as a "truly conscious being capable of making choices, living among other beings with sensation, experience and desires."[47] As science makes its case and scientists argue among themselves, we know that Hildegard proposed her answer, gained from observation and intuition long before today's scientists debated the topic: "No creature, whether visible or invisible, lacks a spiritual life."

7. Angels

Speaking of consciousness and the extent of its presence in the universe, it seems appropriate to ask questions about those light beings known to human cultures around the world as spirits or angels. Hildegard developed angelology so well that scientist Rupert Sheldrake and I devoted one-third of our book on angels to her work. I so respect Sheldrake's courage in daring to discuss angels, since scientific dogma has resulted in a failure to research the topic. Since today's science has taken the lid off the mechanical universe, it seems to both Sheldrake and myself that it has opened the door to serious discussion of these light beings.[48] Among other teachings, Hildegard instructs us that "the angels lift up their voices to God in praise of the good works of humanity. They continually praise the ever-increasing good works of humankind. They climb onto the golden altar which stands before God's countenance. And from now on they intone a new song to honor these works."[49]

8. Healing Medicine

In Allensbach in southern Germany, there exists the Hildegard Center. This center is committed to carrying on Hildegard's teachings about healing, which she writes about in five different books. The center was started by the late Dr Gottfried Hertzka, who first began practicing "Hildegard medicine" in 1965. Dr Hertzka was a medical doctor in Germany who had worked clinically with Hildegard's teachings and authored a best-selling book on her medicine, *So heilt Gott*.

In her writings, Hildegard offers about 2,000 remedies—and Hertzka notes, after years of putting her teachings into practice with patients, that "her medicine works, it *does* heal!"[50] He believes that Hildegard's "natural medicine" can link up with modern medicine. He especially praises Hildegard for her description of the origin and manifestations of cancer, with the precancerous state developing years before cancer is actually diagnosed.[51] His patients are treated preventatively to build up body resistance.

Secondly, Hildegard "explains that detoxification is necessary in order to be healed." There are nutritional poisons, environmental poisons, and mental poisons such as stress, distress, and anger that alter the chemistry of the blood. Hildegard knew these things.

Dr Wighard Strehlow was a research chemist in the pharmaceutical industry before joining Dr Hterzka in his practice at the Hildegard Center in the 1980s. Strehlow credits Hildegard with teaching what today's holistic health movement is remembering: that much sickness is related to imbalances in our souls. Better to look there than to prescribe or pop Prozac.

In his book *Hildegard of Bingen's Spiritual Remedies*, Strehlow stresses Hildegard's sense of the microcosm and the macrocosm, and the healing that comes from a Cosmic Christ consciousness. He writes, "The body-soul psychotherapy of Hildegard is radically different from all other psychotherapeutic approaches, as it emphasizes the fact that the human soul not only is localized within human beings but is also interconnected with the entire universe. Our soul is free of time and space—eternal, infinite, all-powerful and divine by nature... No matter how sick and injured our bodies are, our souls are always whole, holy, beautiful, young, and healthy."[52]

Strehlow believes that today's science has confirmed what Hildegard taught about the autonomic nervous system. It isn't robot-like, but "as Hildegard revealed eight hundred years ago: lifestyle affects the so-called autonomic nervous system. Negative feelings such as hate, anger, and fear as well as positive emotions like love, compassion, hope, and joy exert a strong influence" and can cause either health or disease. Prayer, contemplation, and meditation positively affect healing, and he cites Dr Larry Dossey and Dr Herbert Benson for their scientific research on the results from this kind of medicine:

> wounds can heal over time
> blood pressure goes down
> LDL (harmful) cholesterol levels go down and the HDL (good)
>   count goes up
> the heartbeat normalizes
> the immune system rallies to keep infections out, destroying
>   germs and even cancerous cells.[53]

Hildegard teaches that thirty-five positive healing virtues need to balance thirty-five negative risk factors, or vices, that are detrimental to our health. The virtues uplift us and strengthen us, whereas the vices tear us down. This is put forward in Hildegard's opera, "Play of the Virtues." The soul gets lost and sick. Fasting is a remedy for twenty-eight of the vices; other remedies include prayer, solitude, and physical training. "The purpose of Hildegard's spiritual psychotherapy is to achieve personal well-being and the healing of body and soul, which requires knowledge of the thirty-five virtues and thirty-five vices and the healing power of the divine soul." In Hildegard's play, Anima, the soul, remembers her original home and returns to it, where she receives her original white robe again and is reunited with the virtues, healed and saved.[54]

Strehlow observes that "in contrast to the mystical wisdom and knowledge of the East, Western science has in the past few centuries abandoned any spiritual dimension and is responsible for the environmental disasters plaguing this fragile planet... Hildegard's wisdom can heal the split between science and spirituality because it provides a synthesis of science and nature with religion."[55] Perhaps Hildegard's sensitivity to balance in the psyche could also assist with the growing epidemic of obesity in our culture.

Strehlow believes that many of our killer sicknesses today were quite rare among indigenous peoples of the past, but that our current poor nutrition and stress-filled lifestyles, coupled with loss of a spiritual dimension in society as a whole, are deadly. He explains, "We call these civilization sicknesses autoaggressive, meaning we are killing ourselves."[56] The medical profession for the most part ignores them, Strehlow feels. Hildegard did not.

In this chapter we have witnessed Hildegard interacting with today's scientists around topics of cosmological awareness, light and cosmic religious feeling and intuition, values and conscience, science and imagination, interdependence and compassion, consciousness, angels, and healing medicine. Judging from her passionate interest in such matters, one can only imagine how eager she would be to be engaged in dialog today—and how grateful she must be to be included with her insights and findings.

Chapter 6

HILDEGARD'S LINEAGE

Creation Spirituality and
the Rhineland Mystic Movement

Our sister Hildegard is so special a woman, so unique a force—and yet she didn't drop out of the sky. She belongs to a tradition, a deep lineage in the Jewish and Christian faiths. This lineage is called "creation spirituality," and it's the oldest tradition in the Bible, as well as the tradition from which all wisdom literature comes. Indeed, biblical scholars tell us that Jesus came from the wisdom tradition, which means that creation spirituality was the worldview of the historical Jesus.

This tradition doesn't begin with human sin—and certainly not "original sin," since no Jew, including Jesus, every heard of "original sin." Creation spirituality is a tradition of Original Blessing, and blessing is the theological word for goodness.[1] It's the tradition of original goodness, original grace—or, one might also say as Hildegard does, "original wisdom." Benedict, the 5th century monk who established the Benedictine monastic order to which Hildegard belonged, was also creation-centered in his theology.

Hildegard doesn't only belong to this tradition, but she is also a profound carrier of it. She has been referred to as "the first major German mystic,"[2] and as such she deserves the title of the "Grandmother of the Rhineland mystic movement." The Rhine River in Germany has been called "the Ganges of the West" because so much spiritual energy arose around it over a period of many centuries.

Let me share some of the most prominent names of those I consider to be "Rhineland mystics." Some are more literally from the Rhine than others, though all have deep spiritual roots in the Rhineland. In chronological order, they are: Hildegard (1098-1179), Francis of Assisi (1182-1226), Thomas Aquinas (1225-1274), Mechtild of Magdeburg (1210-c.1282) and many other Beguines, Meister Eckhart (1260-1329), Dante (1265-1321), Julian of Norwich (1342-c.1416), and Nicolas of Cusa (1400-1464).

The Rhineland mystics are characterized by their love of creation, and hence a deep awareness of the Cosmic Christ.[3] Much of this love of creation and its sacredness came from the Celts, who settled all along the Rhine, down into Switzerland, and even into northern Italy, whence comes Francis of Assisi's Rhineland connection. Aquinas and Eckhart both studied in Cologne with Albert the Great, an Aristotelian scientist, alchemist, Dominican friar, and theologian—and, of course, Cologne is on the Rhine. Cues is a small town on the Rhine not far from Bingen.

Only Julian seems to be out of place, since she was an English woman and hermitess locked into a small chamber attached to a church in the town of Norwich. How, you ask, can she be called a "Rhineland mystic"? Not by geography, but by theology. When Meister Eckhart was condemned a week after he died, his Dominican brothers saw to it that many of his works were smuggled into the lowlands—into Spain where he influenced John of the Cross, and into England often under the cover of John Tauler, his student. Julian knew Meister Eckhart well. Dominicans were prominent in Norwich in the 14th century, which was a hotbed of mystical activity. For example, Eckhart says "isness is God," and Julian says "Goodness is God." It's for this reason that an argument can be made that Julian deserves to be called a Rhineland mystic. Hildegard deserves to be called "grandmother" because she's the elder behind so many of these spiritual geniuses.

People sometimes ask me, "Where did you first learn of Hildegard?"

I respond that it was studying Meister Eckhart that led me to Hildegard. I had heard her name from my mentor, Pere Chenu, in his book *Nature, Man and Society in the Twelfth Century*, and I noticed that Thomas Aquinas occasionally referred to her; but my actual interest in finding her was peaked while studying Eckhart. I said to myself, "There's another spirit at work here behind Eckhart in addition to Thomas Aquinas; it feels like a woman is at work in his writings." This is what led me to chase Hildegard down.

The lineage of Hildegard and other Rhineland mystics is deeply Celtic and therefore also deeply Hindu, for many scholars agree today that the Celts came from India. Some of the common themes between Celtic and Hindu theology include an appreciation of the Divine Mother, a deep awareness of the sacredness of matter, non-dualism, an emphasis on birthing and creativity, and a joy-oriented spirituality.[4] Says Eckhart, "I will tell you something I have never said before: God enjoys him/herself. God enjoys all creatures not as creatures but as God."[5] The Chandogya Upanishad of India says, "Where there is joy, there is creating. Know the nature of joy. Where there is the Infinite, there is joy."[6] In many respects Hildegard isn't just living in the 12th century, for ancient chthonic images (images connected with the underworld) emerge in her paintings as well as her verbal images. All these elements and more one can find in Hildegard and these other Rhineland mystics.

Let me say a little more about creation spirituality. The Caribbean poet Derek Walcott, who won the Nobel Prize for literature in 1992, remarked in his acceptance speech, "The fate of poetry is to fall in love with the world in spite of history." I think that's the fate of all art—not just poetry, but music, theater, film, and dance. I think it's also the fate of mystics. The mystic is one who falls in love with the world in spite of history. That is creation spirituality—to fall in love with creation, which isn't the same thing necessarily as human history, thank God! Hildegard is that kind of a mystic. She's absolutely on fire, and her fire is—in her own words—the Holy Spirit. She is on fire with love of the world, with love of creation. You can feel her fire in her music, her images, her words.

I have devoted my life to recovering the creation spirituality tradition because, even though it's the oldest tradition in the Bible, the tradition of Jesus, and the tradition of the greatest mystics of the church, it's little known. Most Christians know only the fall-redemption tradition of original sin that St Augustine articulated in the 4th century—a tradition whose patriarchal pessimism has been carried to extreme lengths by such individuals as John Calvin, who in the 16th century said we are all "depraved beings." If we are to renew Christianity, we must begin with the deep, rich tradition of creation spirituality.

The fall-redemption version of spirituality named the journey as one of: 1) purgation, 2) illumination, and 3)union. The creation spiritual tradition consciously replaces this naming of the journey—which isn't Jewish and isn't biblical—with the *Via Positiva, Via Negativa, Via Creativa,* and *Via Transformativa.* Let me demonstrate how Hildegard, who is immersed in the creation spirituality lineage, names and develops these paths.

1. The *Via Positiva* is about our experience of awe, wonder, gratitude, and delight. It's about our falling in love in spite of history, as Walcott put it. Hildegard is such a lover. She says, "All of creation is a symphony of joy and jubilation."[7] Notice how Hildegard is talking about *all* of creation, which shows how she thinks with a cosmic awareness. All of it is filled with "joy and jubilation." Creation isn't neutral; it isn't just "there." It carries bounty, exuberance, delight, joy, celebration, even jubilation.

Consider what Thomas Berry says in the early 21st century: "In the end the universe can only be explained in terms of celebration. It is all an exuberant expression of existence itself."[8] Consider too that the great feminist archeologist, Marija Gimbutas, comes to the conclusion that the "essence of the goddess civilization was the celebration of life." For Hildegard, the whole universe works together. The universe is a "symphony," in that it harmonizes, is interconnected, and is ultimately one. Hildegard knew what a symphony was, since she wrote lots of music. In fact, she named the collection of her songs "Symphony of the Harmony of Celestial Revelations." She is explicit about the relationship between the cosmos and music. For her the universe is diversity within unity producing "resounding melodies." Recently I learned how today's scientists are discovering that black holes actually emit musical tones, but that they are far too subtle for the human ear to pick up. It seems the human mind, at least in Hildegard's case, did indeed pick up on the symphony of the universe!

We have already seen how Hildegard sees creation as a relationship of lover to beloved, Creator to creation—a relationship that includes not just plants, trees, grasses, and birds, but also human beings. As we have seen, she compares creation and Creator to the same love and fidelity with which God binds woman and man together in the sacrament of marriage. Creation is a sacrament. It's holy.

Hildegard says, "God has gifted creation with everything that is necessary." She sounds quite optimistic. She doesn't carry the scars of dualism that the patriarchal lineage of Plato and Augustine carry. Augustine speaks often of how all of nature is fallen, which Calvin picked up on, complaining that "we are all just mud inside and out." Hildegard has a *via positive*, for she connects nature and grace. Eckhart said "nature is grace," and Julian of Norwich in the 14th century says simply, "Nature is grace, grace is nature." This is an echo of Hildegard, who derives so much juice (one of her favorite words!) from nature.

I mentioned earlier how Hildegard reports several times that she had a vision of the cosmos and a beautiful young lady, and this lady is love. Thus the cosmos is built on love. This vision of a young beautiful woman who is ordering the universe with love, and whose name is love, kept reoccurring to Hildegard. This is a theology of Original Blessing. Reread the passage at the beginning of the Introduction: No fuller expression of Original Blessing has ever been written by a theologian. To speak of Original Blessing doesn't mean one never talks of original sin. Hildegard does talk about original sin. But Original Blessing obviously preceded all sin.

Hildegard calls Mother Mary "the ground of all being."[9] To call Mary the ground of all being is Celtic. Remember that Hildegard was in a Celtic monastery because the Celts settled along the Rhine, and the Celts had a tradition that the earth, the ground of being, the ground of the earth, is the Goddess. In fact, when the Celtic king was crowned, he had to swear an oath of marriage to the Earth. He had to marry the earth. Hildegard praises Mary as the "mother of all joy." Thus joy is a priority for Hildegard. A fullness is found in Mary.

As we saw in chapter three, Hildegard says on numerous occasions, "God is life." To say that God is life is another affirmation of the *via positiva*. Hildegard explains Adam's fall in the Garden of Eden in this way: Adam's sin was a failure in eros, a failure to drink in deeply the beauty and the *grace* of our being here. A failure in the *via positive*—a sin of omission, not commission.

The *via positiva* is about the cataphatic God, "cataphatic" meaning "drawn to the light." This is the God of light. Light, as we have seen, is extremely important to Hildegard and the reason she calls her visions "illuminations." They were moments of enlightenment for her. She talks about the "living light" that has come to her, speaking to her in her visions, even back to the time she was five or six years old. Hildegard is absolutely explicit about her experiences of this living light that comes to her, and that talks and takes on different forms and shapes. She was special in that regard. Light was so important to her and actually spoke to her, as we saw in chapter 2.

2. The *Via Negativa* names our experience of the apophatic divinity, the divinity of darkness and mystery. The path of the *via negativa* includes silence, darkness, and also suffering. Our response on this path is always one of letting go and letting be. Hildegard asks, "Who is the Trinity? You are music, you are life, you are alive in everything, and yet you are *unknown to us*."[10] This is the *via negativa*. The Trinity is music and alive in everything, and yet unknown to us. This is the mystery dimension or the apophatic divinity.

Whenever Hildegard is speaking of the *unknowability* of divinity, she is speaking of the *via negativa*. It's about mystery more than history. She says, "no one can fully grasp the Godhead, which is without beginning and is not subject to origin."[11] No created thing can "completely grasp God's mysteries"[12] and "God cannot be seen but is known through the divine creation...just as the inner brilliance of the sun cannot be seen, God cannot be perceived by mortals." God says. "I remain hidden in every kind of reality, hidden as a fiery power. Everything burns because of me, in such a way as our breath constantly moves us, like the wind-tossed flame in a fire."[13] Like fire, the "hidden God" kind of smolders, then breaks through. Hildegard is honoring the hiddenness and darkness of divinity.

Hildegard further talks about the stillness of God when she says, "Truly the Holy Spirit is an unquenchable fire. It bestows all excellence, sparks all worth, awakes all goodness, ignites speech, enflames human-kind. Yet in this radiance is a *restorative stillness*."[14] In spite of all her images of the fire of creativity and the inflaming of humankind, there's a stillness, and this stillness restores and refreshes.

Notice how Hildegard is balancing yang energy (fire) with yin energy (stillness). "It is a stillness that is similarly in the will to good. It spreads to all sides. The Holy Spirit, then, through one's fervent longings pours the juice of contrition into the hardened human heart."[15] She experiences stillness as something lurking behind our desire to do good, and she envisions it spreading and expanding out. It's everywhere, and it accom-plishes great things such as softening hard hearts.

The *via negativa* includes struggle. Late in life Hildegard confessed to having endured much when she wrote, "I was often severely hindered by sickness and involved with heavy sufferings that threatened to bring me to death's door. And yet God has always made me alive again, even to this day."[16] She had her dark days, and when she talks about them, she puts the story powerfully: "Where am I, a stranger? In the shadow of death. And by which way do I go? In the way of error. And what consola-tion do I have? What strangers have." The soul wanders as a lost stranger while it's busy trying to set up its tent, trying to set up its house of wisdom.

It speaks: "I ought to be a companion of the angels because I am the living breath which God sent into dry dirt, whence I ought to know God and to understand him. But alas! Adders, scorpions, dragons, other serpents hiss at us... Terrified, I sent out the greatest shriek, saying, 'O Mother, where are you? I would suffer pain more lightly if I had not felt the deep pleasure of your presence earlier. Where is your help now?'" Her cry goes out to her Mother as she reaches out for some compassion: "Then I heard the voice of my Mother saying to me, 'O daughter, hurry, for wings have been given to you for flying from the most powerful of all givers, to whom nothing is strong enough to resist. Therefore fly quickly over all these opponents.'"[17]

But still Hildegard continues to sink into a kind of dark night of the soul: "I send forth huge lamentations, and I say, 'O God, you created me, did you not? Behold, the vile world oppresses me.'" Then she says to herself, "I must remember. Now is a time for remembering—for remembering goodness." She is teaching that when you are in the darkness, when you are in depression, you have to call on the *via positiva* again and remember it.

◆

"I send forth huge lamentations, and I say, 'O God, you created me, did you not? Behold, the vile world oppresses me.'...I must remember. Now is a time for remembering—for remembering goodness."

◆

One century later, Mechtild of Magdeburg, who was a lay member of the Beguine movement, the women's movement in the Middle Ages—not a nun, not a married person, but a beguine—talks about how there are times when the lantern goes out, and when even the *memory* of the light of the lantern goes out. She recorded that experience 300 years before John of the Cross wrote about the dark night of the soul. This is what Hildegard is talking about here, too. Yes, illuminations happen, but also darkness happens. In times of darkness, you have to dig into your soul for strength, and you have to dig into your memory for the lantern, which is the *via positiva*. Ultimately this passage of Hildegard's ends when she declares, "Thus I do know the goodness, the goodness of God."[18] And she is calmed.

Life's journey can be difficult. Hildegard paints pictures of having to ford a river and wrestle with demons and crocodiles—the reptilian brain, which is so reactive. Her life wasn't easy. A Jungian therapist with whom I shared one of Hildegard's paintings, which has a great dark figure in it, said to me, "This is the most mature person I've ever met."

I asked him, "Why do you say that?"

He explained, "Look with what frankness and honesty she deals with the shadow in her life and in our collective existence."[19]

While Hildegard isn't in denial of darkness or suffering, it's really amazing how unpreoccupied Hildegard is with the theology of the cross. The fact is that the cross wasn't a significant symbol in Christianity until the 4th century when Emperor Constantine converted to Christianity and waged war, using the cross as a symbol. After all, the cross and crucifixion were part and parcel of the Roman Empire, not of Christ's teaching.

I mentioned earlier that Hildegard actually says we were redeemed by the *incarnation but awakened by the crucifixion.*[20] This means we are redeemed when we find the divine in nature, becoming flesh, which is the meaning of incarnation. I have never seen the cross anywhere standing by itself in Hildegard's paintings. In one instance she paints the crucifixion with blood and water flowing out of Christ's side into a chalice held by a woman who represents the church, and from that chalice a golden stream of light pours into the bread and wine on the altar.[21] The crucifixion doesn't stand alone for Hildegard, which is quite remarkable. Rather, she sees it as a creative moment of starting things over, and of the flowing of grace. But I want to emphasize that she actually says we are redeemed by the incarnation.

Hildegard paints the void in a marvelous mandala in which she presents nine concentric circles of angels—although a few of them are human beings.[22] She mixes angels and human beings in concentric circles. In the very middle of the painting, there's an empty space, a hole, like a donut. She comments, "The innermost circle is empty. It is a full emptiness, the path of transcendence." In other words, the hole is a mirror of fecund nothingness.

The number ten traditionally symbolized the return to unity and the totality of the universe. So in this painting, Hildegard is painting nothingness as the center of all these angels, the nine choirs of angels and humans, singing divine praises. But the middle is the void. She also makes mention of the "secret quiet" that occurs when Wisdom goes inward and heavenly inspiration arrives.[23] Hildegard is in no way out of touch with the void and the nothingness—indeed, all of the elements of the *via negativa*. Thus Hildegard carries the several dimensions of the *via negativa*: stillness, mystery, emptiness, suffering, grief. She teaches letting go and letting be.

3. The *Via Creativa* is the path of creativity. Hildegard is an Olympic champion at the *via creativa*. Her life is a living witness to creativity—so much so that she can be said to be an incarnation of creativity. Let me name some of her creativity.

Hildegard's Creativity at Work

Hildegard's music is exceptional. Since her music came into its own a few years ago, she has been outselling all kinds of pop stars! To share with you just a few observations from a musician about Hildegard's music and how unique it is, Brendan Doyle taught Hildegard's music in our master's program for years; one of our courses was singing her music. Time and again during the first week or two of class, students dropped out because they fainted or came close to fainting while singing this music. It takes so much air to sing her music that you either get high or you faint! People who stayed in the class would come to me after the class and say, "I'm so high!" Those who couldn't quite take it dropped out. Hildegard's music is so demanding, it literally gets you high on air! The image I have of her Gregorian chant is a roller coaster, because it takes you on such a wild ride.

Doyle writes, "Her compositions are incredibly physical. Singing her music comes close to hyperventilation at times." Of course, Hildegard writes about the spirit as wind and breath, so devising a rigorous spiritual practice like singing her music was an important "art as meditation" discipline in her monastery. Doyle comments, "Her music takes you to the extreme of your vocal potential."

Doyle observes that "through the Middle Ages, musical composition was based upon seven modes while in modern times we rely on only two, Aeolian and Ionian, our minor and major keys. A medieval composition was written in one of these modes, but Hildegard's cosmos could not be limited to one mode. In the course of one of her songs, she is likely to jump ahead 500 years and move into another mode." By skipping modes in the middle of her songs, she is "creating whole new worlds of feeling."

Doyle believes that Hildegard actually anticipates Haydn and Mozart because she creates a thematic development in the music as well. For example, she will create a theme around the topic of *viriditas*, or greening power, which moves in and out of her song, just as you get with these much later musicians. Doyle concludes that "her melodies are as memorable to me as a melody of Mozart or Mahler—romantic in their wholeness and vast in their expansiveness. Her music is unique for its time and, I am tempted to say, for any time."[24] Her music is absolutely outstanding, and I call it "erotic Gregorian chant."

Professor Barbara Newman calls Hildegard's music "difficult" and "sui generis," the work of a "maverick" that sounds "either primitive or unnervingly avant-garde." One eccentric feature of Hildegard's style is its wide vocal range: "Many songs have an ambitus of two octaves and some even of two and a half, placing a considerable strain on the voice of the average singer." She scurries "rapidly up and down the octave... several times in the space of a word."[25]

Of course, Hildegard was a poet, because she wrote the lyrics for her music, including the libretto for her *Ordo Virtutum*, which is a morality play set to music. As mentioned in chapter 1, it's the first opera we have in the West, hundreds of years earlier than any other opera. She wrote poetry for her many songs, created theater, and staged her opera with her sisters playing the parts of the virtues and her monk secretary playing the part of the devil. Her poetry too has been called unique, for "no formal poetry written in the twelfth century, and none that Hildegard might have known, is very much like hers," according to Newman. "Nowadays we would call it free verse."[26]

This is especially striking in light of the recent research on Walt Whitman and how his "invention" of free verse 700 years after Hildegard was in fact a *shamanistic practice* he utilized as a "technique of transport" to put both the poet and the reader into an altered state of consciousness.[27] Newman calls Hildegard's poetry, while conventional in topics, "wholly original in her treatment and style," leaving "an indelible impression of freshness and power." Her images "leap out of their verbal wrappings to assault the mind... Startling at first, even incoherent, they slowly or suddenly explode into sense..."[28]

As for her thirty-five paintings, we aren't sure whether she actually executed them or dictated the images to her sisters who executed them. Surely she oversaw the renderings of her visions. I reproduce a collection of her paintings, many of which are mandalas, in my book *Illuminations of Hildegard*. Jung, who was touched by Hildegard and knew her work well, points out that the mandala isn't just a painting but a healing device. So in that sense Hildegard is a healer through her paintings in addition to her advice about medicinal plants and practices.

Hildegard is also a writer. Her first book *Scivias*, which means "Know the Ways"—know the ways of wisdom versus the ways of folly—isn't just a book, for it contains numerous paintings of her visions and ends with her opera. That she couldn't be contained by words is fascinating, for she was bringing the feminine dimension of *process*—such as painting, singing, and theater—into a book. Why restrict books just to words? That's kind of boring! Why not throw in an opera and twenty-eight paintings of visions? She wrote two other books based on powerful visions, *The Book of the Rewards of Life* and *The Book of Divine Works*. The latter also included visions and images. She also wrote two medical works known as *Physica* and *Causae et curae*. The former contains chapters on plants, elements, trees, stones, fish, birds, animals, reptiles and metals—all with the overriding theme of how they can be used for medicinal purposes. We're told that Hildegard "enjoyed a reputation as a healer," which was "a traditional role for women, and especially for nuns, who grew therapeutic plants in their cloister gardens." She is also credited with an act of exorcism of a young noblewoman from Cologne who had been possessed by the devil for eight years. Following on the success of that ritual, the freed subject joined Hildegard's community.[29]

Additionally, Hildegard was an architect, since she helped to design her buildings. When she moved out of the men's monastery, she took her sisters *and* their dowries with them—and we have letters from the abbot, begging her to come back *with* their dowries, which she didn't bother to do! In her monastery she had running water and toilets, which they didn't have back in the men's monastery. With money from her family, she hired 200 Cistercian monks who were the crème de la crème of professional craftsmen for church and cloister construction in her day. We're told she took the blueprint of her cloister from the vision of the city of Jerusalem described in the Bible (Revelation 21:2). It was erected on S. Rupert mountain in Bingen, where it stood until it was destroyed in the thirty years war in the 17th century.

Hildegard was a tremendous letter writer, and we have over 300 of her letters still. Preaching, too, was part of her creativity. She preached all over Germany, which constituted "another highly irregular activity for a woman." Her first preaching tour took her along the Main River. She then preached along the Moselle and Saar rivers. For a third tour, she went along the Rhine, while a fourth took her to the Danube. During these tours, she preached to monks, nuns, secular clergy, and the public. Her basic theme was the laziness of the clergy and their lack of zeal.

What Hildegard's creativity amounts to is that when we are dealing with her in her multiple *via creativa* incarnations, we are dealing with a force! Listing Hildegard's creative work is almost exhausting in itself. Truly it's astounding, because it isn't just the breadth of what she did, but the depth of it—the quality of her music, for example, and her writing, images, and medicinal arts. But she doesn't take credit for all of her work. Rather, she sees herself as an instrument of the artist of artists.

In a beautiful passage about her experience as an artist—and many of us have no doubt had this experience at some time—she says, "The marvels of God are not brought forth from oneself. Rather, it is more like a chord, a sound, that is played. The tone does not come out of the chord itself but rather through the touch of the musician. I am, of course, the lyre and harp of God's kindness."[30] In other words, she sees herself as a mere instrument being played by the Holy Spirit.

The *via creativa* is such an important theme for our survival as a species today. It's clear, I think, to anyone who is half awake that we have to reinvent everything. Education isn't working. Economics aren't working; Main Street has been abused by Wall Street—abuse that continues apace. Religion isn't working. Politics are in chaos. In other words, we have a lot of creating to do. The worst thing we can do is collapse out of inertia, despair, or cynicism. What we have to do is to whip up some of the creativity that drove Hildegard so powerfully!

4. The *Via Transformativa* names the fourth path of the spiritual journey according to the creation spiritual lineage. This is a path of compassion and justice, which is a prophetic path. As I said earlier, the mystic goes through the *positiva*, the *negativa*, then develops the *creativa*, and the prophetic passage is here in the *transformativa*. William Hawking, the American philosopher, says, "The prophet is the mystic in action." So Hildegard was both contemplative and activist, mystic and prophet. Rabbi Heschel explains that the prophet's primary work is *to interfere*. The prophet cares passionately about justice. Hildegard does a lot of interfering. This is clear in her letters, preaching, and writing, where she is a loud trumpet of justice.

◆

"The marvels of God are not brought forth from oneself. Rather, it is more like a chord, a sound, that is played....I am, of course, the lyre and harp of God's kindness."

◆

Hildegard teaches that compassion is the imitation of God and that wisdom gives birth to compassion. So compassion is a big part of her entire consciousness—as is justice, for justice is "God's work." In chapter five we saw her teaching on the interconnectivity of all things; but since interconnectivity is the basis of compassion, this teaching too feeds her commitment to compassion. Relation, not thing-ness, is the essence of all that exists. Compassion is about relation—about sharing joy, sharing grief, and working to relieve one another's pain.

Hildegard, like every prophet, isn't without moral outrage. She is outraged by the treatment of the earth, and she is outraged by corruption in the church of her day—even in the highest places of the church—and doesn't hesitate to express herself on both issues. She also addresses kings and emperors in blunt language. She stands up and she speaks out, a trumpet sounding a wake-up call. She has found her voice—her fifth chakra isn't gagged—and she calls us to find ours. She teaches us to cut through denial and speak truth to power, even if we must pay a price for it.

Regarding ecological injustice, we have heard her warnings in chapter four. They are strong, even fierce, issued in language that would be provocative even for our day—perhaps especially for our day.

Regarding church corruption, we will hear her out in chapter eight. Suffice it to say for the moment that what she has to say demonstrates how deeply involved she is in the *via transformativa*—especially when we consider that German theologian Osiander, a theologian in Nuremburg who took Luther's side in the 16th century Reformation, called Hildegard "the first Protestant." Yes, she was a protester who protested to popes, archbishops, bishops, and abbots. She tells the pope he is "surrounded by evil men" when she writes him directly: "O man, you who sit on the papal throne, you despise God when you don't hurl from yourself the evil, but even worse, embrace it and kiss it by silently tolerating corrupt men. The whole earth is in confusion on account of the ever-recurring false teaching whereby human beings love what God has brought, to nothing. And you, O Rome, are like one in the throes of death."[31] You can see why Luther's men were eager to adopt Hildegard as a sister. This may be one reason for the tardiness of her canonization.

Hildegard wasn't the only one calling for church reform in the 12th century. Bernard of Clairvaux was trying to reform the monks, because the monks were excessively successful and living high on the hog. Francis of Assisi, who came right after Hildegard, also protested, seeking to reform the church. He experienced a powerful dream in which he was told, "Rebuild my church." At first he took to this to mean rebuild a little chapel down the road, which he went and worked on. Then it grew on him that something bigger needed changing, which is when he started his band of brothers and sisters. Dominic, too, a contemporary of Francis, sought to reform the church and to move its educational center from the monastic establishment, married to the feudal country-side, to the new university movements in the cities. So there were many efforts at reformation, but Hildegard was out front and a leader in her own right.

Hildegard talks often of how Christ was a "spiritual warrior" and how we need to be the same. Be "strong like a tree," she repeats often—and I have the impression she's sometimes talking to herself when she invokes this mantra for strength and stamina. All prophets, all warriors, need courage and stamina. She writes, "Oppose the devil like a strong warrior opposes his enemy. Then God is delighted with your struggle, wishes you to call upon God constantly in all hours of your distress."[32]

Each of us is meant to be a strong warrior, which is why Hildegard urges, "Resist strongly. Become a tree. Just as the soul is in the body, the sap is in a tree, the soul passes through the body just like sap through a tree."[33] So it's your soul's strength that she's calling on to give birth, to make these choices that we need to make today as a species if we are going to survive, and if we are going to recreate everything from economics to education and politics. Yes, Hildegard knew the *via transformativa* intimately. She is a warrior calling us to be the same.

We have seen how Hildegard fills out the four paths of creation spirituality with depth, richness, originality, and courage. She is a creation-centered mystic and prophet of the highest order, a stellar representative of the creation spirituality lineage.

Chapter 7

WILD WOMAN AND SHAMAN PROCLAIMING WISDOM, CREATIVITY, AND THE HOLY SPIRIT

Hildegard Meets Dr Clarissa Pinkola Estes

Jungian psychologist Clarissa Pinkola Estes wrote a great and earth-shaking spiritual tome on the return of the Wild Woman some years ago. As I return to that book, I see Hildegard everywhere. Hildegard and Estes are sisters in the deepest of ways. Let me spell out just a few of them.

Hildegard and the Wild Woman Archetype

Estes teaches that the Wild Woman archetype is found around the world: "No matter by which culture a woman is influenced, she understand the words *wild* and *woman*, intuitively."[1]

Where do we find this Wild Woman? "For some women, this vitalizing 'taste of the wild' comes during pregnancy, during nursing their young, during the miracle of change in oneself as one raises a child, during attending to a love relationship as one would attend to a beloved garden." She also comes "through sights of great beauty." And "she comes to us through sound as well; through music which vibrates the sternum, excites

the heart; it comes through the drum, the whistle, the call, and the cry."[2]
Do we not hear and feel this in Hildegard's music, as well as in her
profound treatise on music? We also feel it in the prophetic way she wrote
to the archbishop who silenced her and her monastery for a year.

Estes continues, "It comes through the written and the spoken word;
sometimes a word, a sentence or a poem or a story, is so resonant, so
right, it causes us to remember, at least for an instant, what substance we
are really made from and where is our true home."[3] Hildegard invites us
into the space of the Wild Woman as we experience this wildness
throughout her writing. Her language generates sounds in our soul. Her
visions also carry the power and the sonorous sounds of the music of the
spheres. To read Hildegard, to listen to her music, to meditate on her
paintings, is to taste the Wild Woman in our midst no matter how many
centuries have transpired between Hildegard's day and ours.

We're talking about true feminine energy, or what Estes calls "the
force which funds all females," a "force that women cannot live
without."[4] Hildegard at work is the Wild Woman at work.

The opposite of the Wild Woman occurs when we lose touch with
"instinctive psyche" and live in a "semi-destroyed" state "where images
and powers that are natural to the feminine are not allowed full development. When a woman is cut away from her basic source, she is sanitized,
and her instincts and natural life cycles are lost, subsumed by the culture,
or by the intellect or the ego—one's own or those belonging to others."[5]

Estes says that when we feel cut off from our "God or Gods," overly
self-conscious, frightened, halt or weak, or mired in inertia, it's because
we're cut off from our instincts. Hildegard wasn't at all cut off from her
instinctive psyche, not at all sanitized, not at all subsumed by her culture,
her ego, or that of others. No inertia, no fear there! She stood up to the
powers of her day, powers of religion and powers of the state.

Because Hildegard was so fully in touch with her Wild Woman, she
brings healing. She calls women and men alike back to their deepest
instincts—those of passion and compassion, wisdom and justice,
creativity and beauty. As Estes comments, "Wild Woman is the health of

all women." Part of healing is learning to find one's voice, to empower our fifth chakra, and to stand up for what one truly stands for. As Estes puts it, "Negative complexes are banished or transformed—your dreams will guide you the last part of the way—by putting your foot down, once and for all, and by saying, 'I love my creative life more than I love cooperating with my own oppression.'"[6] Wasn't this Hildegard's vocation her entire life long? She couldn't not express herself and share her wisdom.

Another dimension of becoming healthy involves connecting to our inherent creativity. Wild woman is "patroness to all painters, writers, sculptors, dancers, thinkers, prayermakers, seekers, finders—for they are all busy with the work of invention, and that is the Wild Woman's main occupation."[7] This names Hildegard for sure. Her muse is the Wild Woman. She is busy about invention without any doubt. She is creativity incarnate.

Another dimension of the Wild Woman is that she "wishes to learn. Those who are not delighted by learning, those who cannot be enticed into new ideas or experiences, cannot develop past the road post they rest at now."[8] Hildegard was always learning, always eager to learn. Her deep curiosity was part of her scientific vocation.

Finally, the Wild Woman archetype "resides in the guts, not in the head... She is the one who thunders after injustice."[9] This too is Hildegard at work. She thunders after injustice whether in society or in the church. We can hear her still.

Hildegard as Shaman?

Thomas Berry says that today our species needs fewer professors and priests, but more shamans. He distinguishes a shaman from a prophet in this way: "The Shaman is more comprehensive in his field of consciousness... The prophet is a message bearer...and the prophet critiques the ruling powers. The Shaman functions in a less personal relationship with the divine. He is more cosmological, more primordial, personally more inventive in the source of his insight and his power."[10] This description fits Hildegard well.

For example, Hildegard's Mariology leaves out a personal piety toward Mary, focusing more on the Cosmic Mary and the archetype of the Divine Feminine than on the person of Mary. Historian Barbara Newman comments, "There is a strikingly impersonal quality in her lyrics: she cared as little for the 'personality' of Mary as she cared for the psychology of Eve. Both women are larger than life, not individuals but cosmic theophanies of the feminine; and the purpose of the feminine is to manifest God in the world."[11] As we have seen, the Cosmic Christ plays a far larger role in Hildegard's Christology than does a relationship with Jesus. Clearly she is more cosmological, more primordial, and more inventive with her insights and her power than most theologians since her day. We still don't know to this day where all her medicinal knowledge came from.

A shaman lives in two worlds at once. Poet and former Dominican Bill Everson calls Jesus "perhaps the greatest of all shamans... Forty days in the desert, the carrying of the cross as a Sun Dance." He continues, "The link would seem to be the Animal Powers. Christ would relate to the Animal Powers that preceded our more sophisticated religious impulses."[12]

Hildegard too is much in touch with the Animal Powers. Time and time again she is visited by animals in her visions; and she paints them, including snakes that frame several of her paintings. She includes images of such creatures as bears, leopards, lions, birds, vipers, scorpions, lobsters, and fish. Many of these beasts speak to her and advise her. She devotes an entire chapter (Book Seven) in her book *Physica* to a discussion of animals and their uses for healing and assistance in our work. She recognizes that birds symbolize "the virtue a person reveals in his thinking when, by his internal premeditation, he reckons many things before they come forth in an illustrious deed." Animals that run on land represent the "thoughts and meditations a person brings to completion in work," as well as spiritual longing. Lions mirror the will of a person, while panthers show "ardent desire." Tame animals that walk on land show "the gentleness of the human being." In short, "animals have in them qualities similar to the nature of the human."[13]

A shaman is one who has undergone deep initiation and emerges to serve and heal the community. Hildegard was such a person. Estes defines an "initiated woman" this way: "To be the keepers of the creative fire, and to have intimate knowing about the Life/Death/Life cycles of all nature—this is an initiated woman."[14] Was there anyone who was busier keeping the creative fire alive than Hildegard? Did Jutta not initiate her over a long and profound period of apprenticeship?

Jungian psychologist Steven B. Herrmann, in an essay entitled "The Shamanic Archetype in Robinson Jeffers' Poetry," gives us further insight into the vocation of the shaman when he writes, "The shamanic archetype is based on a pattern of behavior, an inborn form of perceiving the inner and outer Cosmos that operates in close relation to an effort to heal personal, social, and environmental imbalances." The "aesthetic and healing practices" of the shaman are his/her gift to the community's healing and "requires a proper alignment with the spirit and Nature."[15] One can see in Hildegard's devotion to a Cosmic Christ theology a constant search to align spirit and nature.

Poet Bill Everson speaks to the shaman's ways when he says, "The idea of trance is the basic psychological function of the shaman."[16] We have seen how Hildegard herself was often in a trance state while receiving her visions, and also how she led her nuns into a trance state through singing her demanding music. The work of the shaman indeed!

Herrmann believes that "the musical impulse is at the heart of all ecstatic and epic poetry," and that what flows from the artist healer enables "a poetic image to channel aesthetic and curative energies that seem to emanate from the Cosmos." This description seems to fit Hildegard's work well—recall how we began chapter two with her insistence that all of creation makes melody, and that she was listening to it intently. Her music was of the essence of her message. She tells us that her visions of the "Living Light" also emanate from the cosmos.

One shamanic practice among Native Americans was crystal gazing. Hildegard devotes an entire chapter (Book Four) in her book *Physica* to precious stones, including crystals. She recognizes mountains and rivers as the birthplace of many stones that "contain many powers and are effective for many needs. Many things can be done with them."[17] Their beauty and their power are willed by God to be "held in honor and blessing on earth and used for medicine." She offers many remedies to a variety of sicknesses from epilepsy to spider bites, depression to lunacy, drawing on the help of these stones. As for gazing at them, she writes, "If you are oppressed with sadness, look at an onyx intently, then place it in your mouth. The oppression of your mind will cease." Also, "one who always has beryl with him, who often holds it in his hand and looks at it frequently, is not easily at odds with other people, nor does he dispute, but rather he remains tranquil."[18]

One rich dream common to shamanism is that of the "magic flight," which often includes a large winged bird with a message to tell the people. Hildegard had such a vision; indeed, she committed it to poem, music, and drawing. It's a vision of wisdom taking flight with three wings. She shares it with us:

O moving force of Wisdom, encircling the wheel of the cosmos,
Encompassing all that is, all that has life, in one vast circle.
You have three wings: One unfurls aloft in the highest heights.
The second dips its way dripping sweat on the Earth.
Over, under and through all things whirls the third.
Praise to you, O Wisdom, worthy of praise![19]

It does seem that understanding the "shaman" archetype sheds light on many of Hildegard's gifts to the world.

Champion of Wisdom

Wisdom is prominent in Hildegard's teaching. Her first book, which as I mentioned earlier took her ten years to write, is entitled "Scivias," which means, "Know the ways"—that is, the ways of wisdom versus the ways of folly.

The ultimate wisdom for Hildegard is the way of compassion, the "law of the Samaritan who led the wounded man into the inn." This is the proper preaching of the church, she says, and is the law the church itself must obey. The gifts wisdom brings, she teaches, "are always new and simple and the older they become, the richer they are."[20] To be foolish, the opposite of wisdom, is to "lack motherly compassion. Whoever lacks this dies of thirst," she warns.[21]

For Hildegard, compassion is hands-on. It's something we do or don't do. "Nothing—neither gold nor money, costly stones nor pearls—can hide from me the eyes of the poor who weep because they lack life's necessities," she writes.[22] It's Wisdom who "orders all rightly," while she also sparkles in the waters and ignites the beauty of the plains. "Above all I determine truth."[23]

Recall that Wisdom is feminine in the Bible. I mentioned earlier how biblical scholars agree that the historical Jesus came from the wisdom tradition of Israel. Wisdom is nature-based, and she is cosmic. She "walks the vaults of the sky and the sands of the deep" oceans according to the Scriptures (Eccl. 24:5). She encompasses all that is. She is a "friend of prophets," and she prepares food and sets the table for large numbers of guests.

Wisdom is spoken about in the Bible more often than Abraham, Isaac, Jacob, Solomon, Isaiah, Sarah, Miriam, Adam, or Noah. Only God, Job, Moses and David are treated in more depth than Wisdom or Sophia, yet it's surprising how silent the churches have been about her during the modern era.[24] Only now is this silence being broken. Today scholars such as Marcus Borg remind us that Jesus was a wisdom teacher and that in early Christianity he was considered "wisdom incarnate." The wisdom movement in Israel arrived quite late in its history and more or less inherited the prophetic tradition, which by then had pretty much died down.

◆

"Nothing—neither gold nor money, costly stones nor pearls—can hide from me the eyes of the poor who weep because they lack life's necessities"

◆

So wisdom and prophecy go together. Wisdom is a justice-and-compassion-oriented lineage.

Wisdom or Sophia is "perhaps first of all the One at the heart of the creative act... 'She makes all things new.'" (Wisdom 7.27) She was present at the dawn of creation:

> When God established the foundations of the earth,
> I was by God's side, a master craftswoman,
> Delighting God day after day,
> ever at play by God's side,
> at play everywhere in God's domain,
> delighting to be with the children of humanity. (Proverbs 8: 29-31)

But Wisdom wasn't only present at the beginning of creation. "She is a part of the ongoing creative process," for "she deploys her strength from one end of the earth to the other, ordering all things for good" (Ecclesiasticus 8:34).

All these aspects of wisdom, Hildegard knew deeply. She declares, "How wonderful is the wisdom in the Godhead's heart!"[25] When she names our life journey as "seeking out the wisdom of your heart" and setting up a tent of wisdom, she is echoing the biblical passage that tells us Israel wandered the earth in search of a place to set up its tent (an allusion to the prologue of John's Gospel, as well as an instance of Hildegard calling Jesus and the Word of God wisdom). She's also putting our search for wisdom at the core of our spiritual lives. Wisdom becomes the integration of psyche and cosmos, microcosm and macrocosm, which leads to action—the action of compassion and of creativity, for Wisdom is green and creative.

The Holy Spirit, Source of Creativity

For Hildegard, wisdom is the work of the Holy Spirit. For years I have maintained that Western Christianity has an underdeveloped theology of the Holy Spirit. There has been so much emphasis on the cross, sin, and redemption—and so much exclusion of the God of creation and incarnation—that we rarely get around to the Holy Spirit.

Hildegard has the richest development of theology of the Holy Spirit I've found anyplace, frankly. The Holy Spirit is also the feminine. In the Eastern Church, the third part of the Trinity is the feminine side of divinity. In Judaism, *ruach* or Spirit is feminine—but not so in Latin. In the Greek New Testament, one word for Spirit, *pneuma*, is neuter; but *psuche* is spirit as "breath of life" or "soul," and it's feminine.

Hildegard asks, "Who is the Holy Spirit?" To which she replies, "The Holy Spirit is a burning spirit. It kindles the hearts of humankind. Like tympanum and lyre it plays them, gathering volume in the temple of the soul."[26] As a "balm of all wounds," the Holy Spirit is integral to healing. Hildegard attributes Jesus' healing the leper to "the Holy Spirit" anointing the leper. The Holy Spirit fills Jesus to teach and heal. It calls people to repentance. The Holy Spirit "marveled joyfully at the holy deeds" that Jesus did, while it also established virtue.[27] This Spirit "kisses the flesh" with a touch of greenness when it heals.[28]

Having just named the Holy Spirit as fire, Hildegard now sees it as water: "O Holy Spirit, clear fountain, in you we perceive God, how God gathers the perplexed and seeks the lost. Bulwark of life, shelter of those caught in evil, free those in bondage." If Spirit is water and a fountain, it's therefore wetness and greenness. Water and Spirit, yin and yang.

Hildegard's understanding of the Holy Spirit is that it's all about creativity, no matter how you look at it—whether fire, wetness, or greening. So she says that it's within the vessel of the Holy Spirit that wisdom has made her abode. Wisdom and Spirit go together.

Wisdom, Spirit, and creativity go together so thoroughly that Hildegard tells us wisdom "resides in all creative works."[29] You go to creativity to find Spirit because Spirit is all about creativity. After all, it's Spirit that hovered over the dark waters at the beginning of creation. Thomas Aquinas said about 70 years after Hildegard that "the same spirit that hovered over the waters at the beginning of creation hovers over the mind of the artist at work."[30] This is surely Hildegard's view.

In her final book, Hildegard describes a vision of a Cosmic Wheel in which humans are cultivating the cosmic tree by planting and harvesting crops through different seasons of the year. The cosmic wheel isn't unlike a potter's wheel. Those who study symbols tell us that the symbolism of the tree denotes "the life of the cosmos: its consistence, growth, proliferation, generative and regenerative processes. It stands for inexhaustible life."[31] Hildegard seems to be saying that human ingenuity and creativity carry us up into the work of the cosmos itself—and therefore the work of the Holy Spirit, whose job it is to stimulate the creative imagination and invigorate life and liveliness.

Hildegard, in celebrating creativity and the Holy Spirit, isn't talking mere theory, but practice. She was, as we know, an immensely creative artist. The role of music in her life was especially important to her. Keep in mind that she wasn't just composing songs out of the blue. Her sisters were singing these songs on a regular basis. In her opera, they were playing the roles and singing her songs. She even roped in her secretary, who was a monk, to play the devil in her morality play. He didn't sing, but just walked around speaking because her definition of hell is that it's a place where there is no music.

Hildegard had much to say about how the prophets "composed psalms and hymns to increase the devotion of the hearer," and how "they also invented various musical instruments as sonorous accompaniments. The outpouring of the prophetic spirit could not have happened without musical instruments." She cites King David for his psalm: "Praise him with trumpet sound, praise him with lute and harp, let everything that breathes praise the Lord." And she says, "We have been given all these varieties of musical instruments to be able to sing in joyfulness of the heart."[32] All this she wrote in that famous letter to the archbishop who had silenced her and her music. She also warned him that he would go to a place in the next life where there is no music. One wonders whether this creative way in which she told the archbishop he was going to hell contributed to the lingering process of her canonization, as her protestations for church reform may have. It has taken 800 years for the Vatican to recognize and honor this amazing woman.

Hildegard could hardly stop writing about how important music is to the soul, and how desperate we are to put our deepest experiences into forms of artistic expression. She had illuminations, awakenings, experiences of light that took on many forms, including musical forms. She would hear music and voices, then write down what she heard, just as she saw visions and painted them (or had others paint them). She was so on fire with the "living light" that spoke to her in many languages that she had to find ways to share it. This is surely one reason she was out doing theater, music, painting, and writing books. She is saying that all of us have our visions to give birth to, and we shouldn't hold back from doing so.

Hildegard's very awakening, and the beginning of her literary and theological vocation, occurred when she was languishing in bed sick and depressed at the age of 41, which is when she finally decided to "put her hand to drawing." She paints her conversion experience, and in so doing compares her experience to that of the apostles at Pentecost: a veritable descent of the Holy Spirit upon her life and soul; a veritable awakening or resurrection. Included in her painting are two images of a Hopi corn mother (sic). The Hopi corn mother also symbolizes resurrection and rebirth.[33]

Hildegard's Teachings on Creativity

Hildegard writes, "There is wisdom in all creative works."[34] In her classic book *Centering,* potter and poet M. C. Richards talks about turning the wheel as a spiritual act of centering. This is what we called "art as meditation" in our programs of spiritual education through the years, which proved to be so effective in getting people in touch with the mystic inside them. Art is a form of meditation, different from sitting on a cushion but not necessarily inferior. One might say that in many respects art is the West's yoga, because it takes discipline to do it well and to persevere. Art is a device for focusing and for bringing up what's deep in your soul, whether that be messages of beauty or messages of grief—the *via positiva* or the *via negativa*.[35]

Hildegard's statement that there is wisdom in all creative works means that if we are going to renew education, we will need to move from knowledge factories to wisdom schools. The bridge is creativity. Unfortunately, when there's a budget crunch in our schools, out goes the art department, the theater department, the music department. The cuts we make are the opposite of wisdom, since wisdom is "in all creative works." One reason people are allured by creativity is that the lack of wisdom in our world is obvious, and Hildegard is saying something about how we recover it.[36]

In another teaching on creativity, Hildegard explains, "This is how a person becomes a flowering orchard. The person who does good works is indeed this orchard bearing good fruit. This is just like the earth, with its ornamentation of stone and blossoming trees."[37] So we humans are not only blooming flowers, blossoming trees—we are *orchards*. Hildegard manifests a sense of abundance when she's talking about creativity, and she paints this as well. She sees humans as "co-creators" with God and the rest of nature, who give birth to such things as cities, books, and science. A big part of her sense of the *via creativa* is that we are "flowering orchards" sharing in the fertility of the rest of nature.

A major theological category invented by Hildegard herself is *viriditas*, which in Latin means literally "greening power." Greening was a very, very important category for her, for she lived in the Rhineland, which is a richly green area. One might compare it to Wisconsin, where I'm from, or to Galilee, the green part of Israel that Jesus was from. So much of his teaching came from walking the land of his people. You can see this in the parables he creates, how he was constantly learning from observing nature. Hildegard was very much that way too. She is constantly getting back to "greening power." She even talks about the Holy Spirit as being green, like a green sap inside all of us. We are like trees, she says, and the Holy Spirit is the capacity for juiciness, greenness, and moistness.

Hildegard teaches that the only sin in life is drying up. She wrote this to bishops and abbots, telling them they were drying up, and they should get outdoors more, doing whatever it takes to stay "wet and green and moist and juicy"—in other words, creative. This is very womanly talk. She creates a category about vice versus virtue: vice is drying up, virtue is staying alive, juicy, and creative. Obviously she feels we're all capable of this. Creating isn't just for individuals who are uniquely gifted as artists, but for everyone.

"This vigor that hugs the world, it is warm, it is moistening, it is firm, it is greening," says Hildegard, adding, "This is so that all creatures might germinate and grow." She sees verdancy, viriditas, greening power everywhere. She says, "The earth of humankind contains all moistness, all verdancy, all germinating power. It is in so many ways fruitful. All creation comes from it. Yet it forms not only the basic raw material for humankind but also the substance of the incarnation of God's Son."[38] Here she is linking the *via positiva* and the *via creativa*, doubling down on the idea of divinity taking on flesh, which is a great creative act that we all take on.

"Humankind is full of all creative possibility," Hildegard asserts. "Humankind is God's work. Humankind alone is called to assist God and called to co-create. We can set into creation all that is necessary and life-sustaining."[39] She is confident of our capacity to create and to make a difference. She's certainly an optimist in this regard. But after all, we are all co-creators.

Hildegard sees creativity at the core of our vocation as human beings when she pictures God saying, "I have been moved by the form of humankind, I have kissed it, grounded it in faithful relationship. Thus I have exalted humankind with the vocation of creation. I call humankind to the same norm."[40] We have a *vocation* to create, which is why we are exalted as co-creators. This is our nobility, but also our serious responsibility. Hildegard links her teaching on the Cosmic Christ to our creativity, for "the Word is living, being, spirit, all verdant greening, all creativity."[41] So we see that for Hildegard, greening and creativity are synonyms. Yet it's also the divine presence at work in us both as Holy Spirit and as the Word or the Cosmic Christ. "In the beginning was the word," thus all creativity is preceded by the coming of the Cosmic Christ and the Holy Spirit.

Hildegard says, "There are two aspects to humanity: the singing of praise to God and the doing of good works."[42] The *via positiva* is our praise, while the doing of good works is a combination of the *via creativa* and *via transformativa*. "It is in praise and service that the surprise of God is consummated."[43] You might say we are the surprise—the surprise of God. Hildegard isn't oblivious when it comes to how we can do damage with our powers of creativity, as we saw in chapter four around issues of eco injustice. But she is hopeful we'll make the right choices with our creativity.

Hildegard discusses conditions for creativity and what happens when we go dry, explaining, "When a forest does not green vigorously, then it is no longer a forest. When a tree does not blossom it cannot bear fruit. Likewise, a person cannot be fruitful without the greening power of faith. The soul that is full of wisdom is saturated with the spray of a bubbling fountain, God himself."[44] God is a bubbling fountain, and we drink from that Source, that fountain of creativity, when we give birth. Faith takes us to the source. Hildegard is calling on both the Holy Spirit as fire (yang energy) and as a bubbling fountain (yin energy) to describe the creative process. Sometimes it's the fire of creativity, sometimes the water of creativity, the yang and the yin. They marry, you might say, in the *via creativa*—a sacred and fruitful marriage indeed.

◆

"It is in praise and service that the surprise of God is consummated."

◆

Another condition of creativity for Hildegard is trust. The opposite of trust is doubt, self-doubt—and she knew how the artist struggles with trust. It takes a certain trust to give birth and brave the chaos. She says this time and again. "Trust shows the way," she says, and "with the passion of heavenly yearning, we all produce rich fruit. But it depends on greening love and on the victorious banner that is trust."[45] So trust requires that we come to grips with our uniqueness and the gifts we have to share.

We have seen that creativity and the Holy Spirit muster energy in Hildegard's view of humanity's noble vocation. Rightly, can she be called a living example of the shaman as well as the wild woman archetype. She is with us still, urging us on.

Chapter 8

HILDEGARD AS PROPHET TO SOCIETY AND RELIGION

In considering Hildegard's commitment to the *via transformativa*, we spoke briefly about her efforts to reform religion and society. In this chapter we'll fill in her contribution in greater depth. It's ironic that Hildegard is being canonized and named Doctor of the Church by the current Vatican regime. I frankly do not believe the Vatican, in canonizing her, has a clue what she really stands for!

One wonders, for example, how the present Vatican, having attacked and fired over 102 theologians in the church and calling itself the exclusive "magisterium" or teacher, would respond to Hildegard's teaching when she says, "The best treasure you have is a living intellect"? There's nothing anti-intellectual about Hildegard. She's no fundamentalist by any stretch of the imagination. She wouldn't relinquish her conscience or consciousness to the Vatican or anyone else. If the best treasure we possess is a living intellect, why are the ecclesial patriarchal so-called guarantors of the faith attacking it?

Nor does Hildegard agree that the pope and the curia are the head of the church. Rather, in her theology, Christ and the Word are the head of the church and its cornerstone, while lay people are the "shining stones" of the church. The clergy are present to serve.

One wonders whether the Vatican bothered to read Hildegard's letters to popes, abbots, and kings and queens, or whether they have an inkling of how she put forward a respect for the Divine Feminine that's nowhere found in the past forty years of the history of the church in Rome. To bring in the Divine Feminine, as Hildegard is destined to do, spells trouble of a deep kind for the patriarchal exclusiveness and "male only" club that constitutes the curia and bureaucracies telling Catholic priests, theologians, bishops, and lay people what they can and cannot think and do.

How can there be so little shame in this same curial "boyz" club over the moral and psychological atrocities committed by priests against children, often with the hierarchy knowledgeable of and busy covering up the crimes? What would Hildegard say to this kind of religious malfeasance?

Two recent acts of silliness emerging from the foggy bottom of the often-concealed Vatican bureaucracies include:

1) An examination of Catholic sisters in America accused of being "radical feminists," though with absolutely no definition of the term—a term thrown about wildly by Cardinal Ratzinger when he was Chief Inquisitor. These are sisters who have served needy people generously for decades in the spirit of Vatican II and who, unlike their accusers in Rome, have no pedophile skeletons in their moral closet. Vatican accusers are shameless to be launching such witch-hunts, though of course adept at it since they have been doing similar things to theologians for forty years.

2) We've also learned recently that some American bishops are attacking the girl scouts (sic) for being purveyors of sexual immorality! It's hard to imagine that a boys' club that thinks these kinds of thoughts has a clue about the deeper issues around the Divine Feminine that Hildegard proposes. By canonizing Hildegard, the boyz will have met their match.

Hildegard: Prophet Criticizing Society's Power Elites

Hildegard's critique extended far beyond church boundaries in her day. She wrote Bertha, the Queen of Greece and Empress of Byzantium, a personal letter to "look to the One who has moved you and who desires from your heart a burnt offering, the gift of keeping all of God's commandments. Sigh for the Divine."[1] She wrote King Henry II of England, who was the nemesis to Thomas Becket, murdered in his cathedral at Canterbury in 1170. She also wrote to King Konrad III, who participated in the Second Crusade, which ended in failure, telling him, "Listen: there are certain ways in which you are turning from God. The times in which you live are as frivolous as a gossiping woman. These times, too, tend towards a hostile injustice, which strives to destroy the justice in the vineyard of the Lord... God who knows all these things speaks to you, O king. When you hear this, O man, pull yourself together against your self-will, and improve yourself, so that you may come purified to the times in which you need no more to be ashamed of your days."[2] She urged him to "imitate the highest Judge and Ruler in his compassion," and to be a king for justice and a fighter against injustice. Barbara Newman observes that "in political affairs Hildegard could take advantage of her aristocratic standing and her celebrity to obtain privileges from the great; but she could equally well oppose them, qua prophet, in the name of God."[3]

On his deathbed, King Konrad designated Frederick as his heir, and Frederick was crowned emperor in Aachen in 1152. He's known in history as Barbarossa, and Hildegard wrote him four letters that we still possess. Hildegard and Barbarossa met in Ingelheim in the mid 1150s and exchanged correspondence. Later, when Barbarossa backed a papal candidate, Paschal III, in opposition to Pope Alexander III in Rome, Hildegard was furious about the schism he was endorsing and "sent him a sharp rebuke, comparing him to an infant and a madman." When Paschal III died and Barbarossa named another anti-pope, Hildegard "thundered forth the wrath of God" upon him with these words: "He Who Is says: I destroy contumacy, and by myself I crush the resistance of those who despise me. Woe, woe to the malice of wicked men who defy me! Hear this, king, if you wish to live; otherwise my sword shall smite you." Newman calls these "savage outbursts" from the mouth of Hildegard.[4] She is surely choosing to interfere—and this at the highest levels of civil hierarchy, the emperor himself!

Seeing her passion for justice in the affairs of the world around her, one wonders if today, as in the 12th century, Hildegard challenges—the goddess challenges through her—the entire direction that Western culture is headed, a direction that all too readily ignores the peril of Mother Earth and the peril of women everywhere both in the church and in society. She critiques the lack of the Divine Feminine, the lack of compassion. Since she works from a trust in her own mystical experience, she speaks with authority.

Would Hildegard have something to say about the rape of Main Street by Wall Street and the bailing out of Wall Street by Main Street? Would she have something to say about the fact that CEOs today are receiving 200 times the salaries of their employees and multimillions in compensation, even when they fire employees and move business abroad, while hiding their dollars in offshore accounts? Yes, she would—and does. Greed, she says, leads to trouble: "When the greedy do not get what they want, they fall into a depression from which they are not lightly lifted. The day hurries quickly by, they say, 'it is always night.' If happiness should stand outside, just beyond their door, they say, 'I am accursed.' Should it go well with all they undertake, still they would say, 'it goes badly!' You snakelike, hellish tongues! You dare to live without the verdancy of God's grace."[5]

Hildegard has strong words also for the hard-hearted ones whom she sees in a vision as "dense smoke" with "very large black eyes," who speak thus: "Why should I do any work [for others]? Why should I wear myself out? Nothing excites me except what benefits me directly. Let God who created all things take care of these things... For if I am always busy being compassionate, what good will it do me? What kind of life will I have if I pay attention to all the happy and sad people? I will take care of myself. Let others take care of themselves."[6] Thus speaks the hard-hearted soul of Hildegard's day. Does this sound familiar?

Hildegard explains the large black eyes: "This sin hardens people so much that they do not wish to know the image of God nor recognize it in other people because without kindness they lack any kind of mercy and goodness." While looking to praise, they instead fall into envy, "which is like the poison of a snake" and "drives out all greenness." Hildegard calls this utter lack of compassion and capacity to praise "the worst evil of all evils. It spares no one and shows no mercy. It despises men and draws back from God. It does not rejoice with men nor does it encourage humans to do good deeds. It is very hard and despises all things."[7] She further warns about how excess doesn't satisfy the soul when she writes, "No one is able to be satisfied by abundance—you are only bored by it."[8]

In another vision that very much anticipates Dante's picture of the Inferno, Hildegard
sees the hard-hearted ones tossed into a deep
hole amid spikes and worms and smoke
emitted from "seething pitch." They "were
attacked by the worms because they had
brought inhuman sorrows to others, and they
were attacked by the fiery spikes because they
had been hard-hearted and showed no mercy."
And a "voice of the living light" said to
Hildegard, "These things that you see are true. If those who were so hard-hearted while they had been alive that they showed no mercy to others...let them fast and scourge themselves."[9] Hildegard adds, "Hard-heartedness is the worst sin since it shows no mercy. Neither does it think that charity is necessary nor does it do any good works. Hard-heartedness was strong in tyrants."[10]

Yes, Hildegard would have something to say to injustice and lack of compassion on Wall Street and beyond. Tyrants, she proposes, should begin their repentance by scourging themselves. She sees hard-hearted-ness as "the worst of sins" because it lacks compassion, which is a lack of the mother principle at work. Recall that the words for "compassion" in both Hebrew and Arabic come from the words for "womb."

Concerning the absence of the Divine Feminine and the prominence of a vile patriarchy, consider the following reality. I have a friend who traveled this past month to India to learn, along with several other

◆

**"No one is able
to be satisfied by
abundance—you are
only bored by it."**

◆

individuals including Gloria Steinem, about the sexual trade there. He was shocked to the bottom of his feet. There are entire villages where parents sell their nine-year-old girls into sexual slavery, which is supposedly the only means of economic survival for the families. This has been going on for generations. The brothers of the girls abuse them from the time they are very young with bullying and physical attacks, thus preparing them for lives of servitude. When they get pregnant, often at a very young age, the family prays that they will give birth to a girl so that this new generation of girls too can be sold into sexual slavery.

This is just one more story of the patriarchal goings-on on our planet. It's horrific, and it's happening everywhere in various forms. We need an awakening to the Divine Mother and the Divine Feminine that reestablishes the dignity and rights of women and girls. Men shouldn't sit back and wait for women to carry the fight. Men must stand up to patriarchy, becoming the warriors they were meant to be. This includes patriarchy in the church. Hildegard is a leader for our times. If she could do what she did in the 12th century, she can surely assist us in the 21st.

Hildegard as Prophet Against Church Corruption

Let us hear Hildegard's critique of the church hierarchy of her day. To Pope Anastasius IV, she wrote on July 12, 1153, "O man, the eye of your discernment weakens. You are becoming weary, too tired to restrain the arrogant boastfulness of people to whom you have entrusted your heart. Why do you not call these shipwrecked people back? You are neglecting Justice, the King's daughter, the heavenly bride, the woman who was entrusted to you. Her crown and jeweled raiments are torn to pieces through the moral crudeness of men who bark like dogs and make stupid sounds like chickens which sometimes begin to cackle in the middle of the night. They are hypocrites. With their words they make a show of illusory peace, but within, in their hearts, they grind their teeth like a dog who wags its tail at a recognized friend but bites with its sharp teeth an experienced warrior who fights for the King's house. Why do you tolerate the evil ways of people who, in the darkness of foolishness, draw every-thing harmful to themselves? They are like hens who make noise during the night and terrify themselves."[11] Maybe this is why they're so afraid in the Vatican—they terrify themselves!

Having had my share of interaction with the curia of our day, I would pronounce this a pretty accurate description of the curia in the year 2012. Yet Hildegard is talking about them in the 12th century! Perhaps things haven't changed much in the interim. Where are others talking today with Hildegard's honesty and candor? I see bishops and provin-cials of male religious orders cowering in the corner, hoping not to be noticed; and when they are noticed, they willingly throw overboard some of the most prophetic voices in their orders. An example is Father Roy Bourgeois from the Maryknoll religious order, who for years went to prison as a conscientious objector to the School of the Americas that was training South American soldiers in torture tactics, but is now being run out of the order because he dares to question the way the Vatican is treating women in the church.

◆

"Pope Anastasius, Why do you tolerate the evil ways of people who, in the darkness of foolishness, draw everything harmful to themselves? They are like hens who make noise during the night and terrify themselves."

◆

Hildegard continues in her assessment of the pope: "People who act like this aren't rooted in goodness. You should be doing battle with evil, but that is precisely what you aren't doing, when you don't dig out by the root that evil which suffocates the good. And why not? Because of your fear of the evil men who lay snares in nocturnal ambush and love the gold of death more than the beautiful King's daughter, Justice."[12] How significant is this phrase, which she returns to often, that justice is "the King's daughter"? She explicitly links justice to the feminine, Lady Justice.

Hildegard prophesies hard times for the pope and the group around him when she says, "O man, You will be so shaken that the strength of your feet, the feet on which you now stand, will disappear. For you don't love the King's daughter, Justice...but as in delirium of sleep, you push her away from you. That is why she will flee from you, unless you call her back." And finally: "And you, O man, who have been placed as a visible shepherd, rise up and hasten quickly to Justice, so that you will not be criticized by the great Doctor for not having cleansed your flock from dirt, for not having anointed them with oil."[13]

Notice how great an emphasis Hildegard puts on *justice*. She calls God "the great Doctor." Elsewhere she says, "True love, which follows in the footsteps of the Son of God, tramples upon all injustice...injustice is also dreadful in its very nature, poisonous in its temptations, and black in its abandonment."[14] Is there anything close to justice happening in the Catholic Church today, as it covers up pedophile abuse and lashes out at SNAP, an organization to protect pedophile victims that was created by a man and a woman who were themselves abused by priests as young people? As it covers up for hierarchy, who in turn covered up for pedophile clergy? As it welcomes holocaust-denying bishops into the fold, while silencing and hounding liberation theology bishops—including the saintly Oscar Romero? And as it welcomes Anglican clergy—even married ones— provided they can prove their bona fides with sexist and homophobic credentials? What would Hildegard say to the *present pope*? And the one before him on whose watch all these scandals were exposed, while he stood by and did nothing about it, yet during this time prosecuted a "purge" of all thinking theologians—a purge that continues to this day?

Hildegard's words are a mouthful to write to anybody, much less a pope in the 12th century! In the 21st century you can always quit—just tell the pope to go to hell and leave and join a different church. But in the 12th century there weren't a lot of options! Thus the courage of this woman was amazing. Even with diverse options today, it's rare to hear any kind of criticism addressed to the papacy and to papalolatry compara- ble to Hildegard's in her day.

To Abbot Kuno of Disibodenberg, the monastery she exited with her fellow sisters and their dowries, she writes, "I have heard from the Lord,

'O human being, why do you sleep? Why do you have no taste for the good works that sound in God's ears like a symphony? Why do you not search out the house of your heart and renounce your brazen unruliness? You strike me in the face when you push away my members in their woundedness without looking at me, even though I am the one who draws back to the fold those who wander. You will have to answer for these things in my presence, for the house of your heart and for the city which I created and washed in the blood of the Lamb. Why do you not shrink from destroying a person, since it wasn't you who created him?"[15]

Hildegard wasn't too happy with the way she was treated in that monastery, as is clear from a letter that she wrote the prior: "O Justice, you are without a homeland. You are a foreigner in the city of those who make up fables and choose these over the tasks assigned to them for their own will."[16] One senses that she was smarting somewhat from a hurtful experience of living in that community.

"O Justice, you are without a homeland. You are a foreigner in the city of those who make up fables."

To Philip, the dean of the Cologne cathedral and to the whole clergy of Cologne, she writes, "The Divine Who was and Who is and Who is to come speaks to the shepherds of the Church: 'Beloved sons, you pasture my flocks according to the explicit direction of God's words. Why are you not ashamed, then, when you see how all the other creatures on the face of the Earth don't neglect, but rather fulfill, the directions they have from their Master?... The trumpet of the Lord is the justice of God that you should consider with great zeal in holiness... In your sermons there are no lights in the firmament of God's justice, just as when the stars aren't shining in the sky. You are night, a night which exhales darkness. And you are like a people that does no work and out of inertia fails to walk in the light. You are like a naked snake that creeps into its hole... So now, what do you have to say for yourselves? You have no eyes if your works do not illuminate in the fire of the Holy Spirit... For the sake of this transitory, worldly reputation you let yourselves be crippled. Soon you'll all be soldiers, then slaves, then buffoons. With your empty and silly behavior, you might well be good for nothing more than to scare away some flies in the summer!"[17]

In a letter to Abbot Hellinger, who asked her for help, Hildegard wrote back, "Now listen and learn, so that you blush with shame when you taste in your soul what I now say. Sometimes you have the style of a bear, who often grumbles to itself in secret. Sometimes you have the style of an ass, for you aren't solicitous in your duties but are glum and in many ways bungling as well." He's glum *and* bungling! "That's why there are times when you don't bring the evil of the bear and its godlessness to execution. In a similar way you also have the style of certain birds who belong neither to those who fly high nor to those who fly low, with the result that the higher-flying birds swoop past them overhead and the lower-flying birds cannot harm them.

"To such behavior the heavenly Father gives an answer: 'Your heart grumbles over my Justice. You don't seek the right answer in her, but you harbor in yourself a certain grumbling like that of the bear.'" She is informing the abbot that God is talking to him through her words, and she ends the letter this way: "But I, miserable creature, see in you a plague-black fire ignited against us. That's something you should consign to forgetfulness in good conscience, so that during the time of your office the grace and blessing of God do not leave you. So love the Justice of God, in which you are loved by God."[18]

Hildegard wrote monks in a Swiss monastery telling them, "You who break out in your evil deeds, you were called 'Mountain of the Lord' because you should imitate the Son of God through your cloistered behavior. Why do you transgress the Motherly inner realm of love and modesty the way you are doing? Alas, what pain over this misery..."[19]

From Hildegard's correspondence, one gets a taste of her prophetic anger and a deep awareness of what her preaching must have been like. Indeed, at the end of her excoriating letter to the priests of Cologne, she puts in a personal note about her travels and contacts: "I am but an anxious and poor woman, who for two years was driven to represent this matter personally to teachers, professors, and other learned people in the prestigious places where they live. But because the Church was in schism, I have given up this preaching."[20] In her fury at church corruption, she doesn't hold back. Keep in mind that it wasn't as easy in that day as writing an email is today. She would write these things, mail them, and someone had to go on a boat and/or horseback and deliver them, which meant correspondence wasn't swift. It was no doubt something of an event to receive a letter from Hildegard.

A number of abbots and others wrote her asking for her counsel personally or for their community. Hildegard addressed the role of priests on many occasions, especially when she preached. She was invited to preach often, whereas in today's church women are forbidden to preach. She warns clergy not to succumb to boredom, jealousy, or dryness, and that they should constantly be reforming themselves. They should "walk through the way of justice." For if they lack the "fervor of justice," they will bear no fruit. Sterility, not creativity, occurs. "The winds fly, and the noise of the winds resounds, but the roots do not flourish or the seed produce anything," she warns. Lots of air, but no substance. Lots of noise, but no fruit. She admonishes clergy not to shout like useless, dry dust, but to put on a new man and be green. She calls priests to their vocation as prophets who speak on behalf of justice: "Neither angels nor priests nor prophets will conceal the justice of God. Rather they are to bring it forth."[21] She urges the clergy to work for a living and not "live by the altar," that is by taking stipends for religious ceremonies exclusively.

Hildegard breaks into apocalyptic imagery when she predicts the future of church corruption, painting a picture of a monster taking over the church. Human dung spreads over the church. Moving with "monstrous ugliness it spread a foul stench on the mountain," while tearing "the institution of the church to pieces with the crudest greediness. Bloody wounds appear on the thighs of mother church." Who is this monster? It is "the antichrist, the son of injustice, the cursed one of the cursed ones." Death rushes into the church because "faith staggers in people and the Gospel limps in some people..." She complains, "The divine Scriptures have been rendered lukewarm." And she addresses the monster: "O you cave of injustice...your works seek the pit of hell. You will lie absorbed in your gluttony there and that hellish place will vomit forth stink. The world will recognize in this stench the bitterness of death in the destroyer of destructions." Moreover, this "worst of beasts" joins up with kings, dukes, leaders, and those with money and prestige, while he covers up the power of the inner person to see truth. Her picture of this beast includes a graphic penis extended into the crowd of corrupted men.[22]

One might wonder whether this graphic portrayal doesn't help to name in vivid imagery a time like ours when the church has sold its soul to fascist powers and power brokers like Opus Dei, Legion of Christ, Communion and Liberation, the CIA, media moguls, and other destroyers of gospel-driven movements such as base communities and theologies of liberation that address authentic needs of the poor and oppressed.

For Hildegard, the chief cornerstone of the church is Christ, and the people are the "living stones" that make up the church—living because they work for justice and compassion. It's the lay people, she says, "who adorn the church of God the most." These people "embellish the church greatly."[23]

Hildegard stresses that it's the lay people's love for one another in marriage that brings forth sons and daughters to people the church and make it green, youthful, and alive.[24] For Hildegard, marriage is primarily a union of husband and wife, a union of love. This teaching was quite rare in her day. She celebrates both the contemplation and the procreation that male-female relationships engender. She writes, "When Adam looked at Eve, he was utterly filled with wisdom, for he saw the mother through whom he would beget children. But when Eve looked at Adam, she gazed at him as if she were seeing into heaven, as a soul that longs for heavenly things stretches upward, for she set her hope in the man."[25] This is an amazing passage about human love and the beauty and hope it arouses.

Newman adds that Hildegard presents a surprising "strong erotic sensitivity" and was "neither naive nor prudish."[26] Writing about marital sex, she says that the man "is like a stag thirsting for the fountain, he races swiftly to the woman and she to him—she like a threshing-floor pounded by his many strokes and brought to heat when the grains are threshed inside her."[27] Quite surprising language for a woman vowed to celibacy! Obviously she was in conversation with laywomen and both counseled and learned from them. She compared man's sexual desire to a "brushfire" and woman's to "continuous but gentle sunlight." This teaching contradicted the accepted wisdom of the time "which held that women were more lustful than men."[28]

In the personal sphere, Hildegard paid a price and suffered from her efforts at reform. When at eighty years of age she was interdicted, the experience was arduous for both her and her community. Newman calls it "the greatest trial of her life."[29] For one thing, it meant neither she nor any of her fellow nuns were allowed to sing the Office or receive the sacraments. This was very difficult for her and them. She wrote to many other bishops, trying to get her bishop to relent, but he wouldn't, remaining stubborn about it for over a year. Yet she refused to compromise over the issue, and she and her sisters were eventually reinstated by the archbishop. She died six months later.

Hildegard not only preached strength, but practiced it. She was strong herself. Part of her strength comes from her life among Benedictine women, as I have often observed that Benedictine women—whose 1,500 year tradition has given them considerable autonomy vis-a-vis masculine dominated church structures—have found within themselves a healthy sense of their masculine side. Hildegard, no less than Sister Joan Chittister today, is a prime example of this kind of inner strength. Hildegard doesn't succumb to fear or timidity. She isn't afraid to "interfere" and do the prophetic work of standing up to society's and religion's injustices. She paid the price that prophets often pay, but didn't wallow in self-pity or recriminations. She invites us to do the same.

Chapter 9

HILDEGARD AS HERALD OF THE DIVINE FEMININE

Hildegard Meets Dorothee Soelle

Hildegard displays at times the energy of both Kali and the Black Madonna, a kind of fierceness. In part, her resilience may have been derived from her Celtic spiritual roots, as one can find this kind of sureness and strength in Celtic women even to this day. It originates from a deep grounding in the Divine Feminine. Accordingly Hildegard writes about Mary as the "ground of all being."[1] Sometimes we talk about God as ground of all being, but she addresses Mary as ground of all being. This is Goddess talk, the language of the Divine Feminine. It is strong.

Hildegard composed a poem in which she says that "God made the form of woman to be the mirror of all his beauty, the embrace of his whole creation."[2] We noted earlier that Hildegard ascribes the work of creation to a woman named Love. In doing this she is advancing the biblical teaching that Wisdom was present at creation.

She describes her vision this way: "I heard a voice speaking to me: 'The young woman whom you see is Love. She has her tent in

◆

"I heard a voice speaking to me: 'The young woman whom you see is Love. She has her tent in eternity... It was love which was the source of this creation in the beginning...She made everything...'"

◆

eternity... It was love which was the source of this creation in the beginning when God said: 'Let it be!' And it was. As though in the blinking of an eye, the whole creation was formed through love. The young woman is radiant in such a clear, lightning-like brilliance of countenance that you can't fully look at her... She holds the sun and moon in her right hand and embraces them tenderly... The whole of creation calls this maiden 'Lady.' For it was from her that all of creation proceeded, since Love was the first. She made everything... Love was in eternity and brought forth, in the beginning of all holiness, all creatures without any admixture of evil. Adam and Eve as well were produced by love from the pure nature of the Earth."[3] This amazing vision, written in a letter to Abbot Adam of Ebrach, pronounces on a theology of original blessing.

Hildegard isn't isolated with the Divine Feminine. There's no sign saying "men need not enter." Because she incorporates masculine energies, she has something for both men and women. This is only natural, since the Goddess is in men as well as in women, and the Divine Mother is in the male as well as the female. It's out of this marriage of the Divine Feminine and the Sacred Masculine that we give birth to what lasts and what matters. I think this is one of Hildegard's messages for us.

I mentioned earlier how Webster's dictionary defines the work of "heralding" as "to give notice of," "to announce," or "to greet with enthusiasm." Hildegard does all this as a *herald of the Divine Feminine*. She gives notice, announces, and greets with enthusiasm. Let me share with you other instances of Hildegard heralding and celebrating the Divine Feminine.

Hildegard and Dorothee Soelle

The late German theologian Dorothee Soelle lived through the Nazi era in her home country. No doubt this had a lot to do with her devotion to liberation theology, including the liberation of women, as well as her suspicion of calls for "obedience."

Soelle was keen on the liberating aspects of the mystical tradition.

She teaches that mysticism is the true language of religion, and stresses, "I do not mean the stolen language in which a male God ordains and imperial power radiates forth." What is her definition of mysticism? "I am completely and utterly in God, I cannot fall out of God, I am imperishable. 'Who shall separate us from the love of God?' we can then ask with Paul the mystic, 'neither death nor life, height nor depth, neither present nor future.' (Romans 8:35 and 38)."[4] Hildegard could surely live with this definition of mysticism.

Soelle also points out that mysticism deconstructs patriarchy, for it "comes closest to overcoming the hierarchical masculine concept of God—a mysticism to be sure, in which the thirst for real liberation does not lead to drowning in the sea of unconsciousness... The mystical certainty that nothing can separate us from the love of God grows when we ourselves become one with love by placing ourselves, freely and without guarantee of success, on the side of love."[5]

Soelle writes that "the goal of the Christian religion is not the idolizing of Christ, not christolatry, but that we all 'are in Christ,' as the mystical expression goes, that we have a part in the life of Christ. This savior is a wounded healer, and he heals so that we may become as he is... Heal the sick, even those who without knowing it have contracted the great neuroses of our society, who know no mercy within themselves and their children when they consent to the nuclear state and technologies minimal to life. To feed the hungry means to do away with militarism. To bless the children means to leave the trees standing for them."[6] Hildegard would surely agree. She is in no way christolatrous, since hers is a Cosmic Christ. She too would seek to heal the great neuroses of our society.

Soelle draws another lesson from the Divine Mother that's congruent with Hildegard's emphasis on the "web of life" of all creation. For her, this is the real meaning of transcendence in a feminist worldview, for "in feminist theology, therefore, the issue is not about exchanging pronouns but about another way of thinking of transcendence. Transcendence is no longer to be understood as being independent of everything and ruling over everything else, but rather as being bound up in the web of life... That means that we move from God-above-us to God-within-us and overcome false transcendence hierarchically conceived."[7] Surely Hildegard does this when she says that "God is life to the fullest"[8] and speaks of the Holy Spirit bringing about the creative "greening power" within us all. Truly she is in touch with this "God within," which constitutes true transcendence.

Feminist archeologist Marija Gimbutas explains that the goddess "in all her manifestations was a symbol of the unity of all life in Nature."[9] When we hear Hildegard talking about "God as life" and the "web of life," we are hearing about the goddess. Hildegard's fierce commitment to examining the microcosm and the macrocosm—not just for the experience of awe, beauty and wonder, but also for the physical, psychological, and communal healing to be found there—is also a celebration of the goddess. A Cosmic Christ theology *is* a feminist theology.

God as Mother, God as Circle

On several occasions Hildegard offers images of the motherhood of God and the circle that is God. She talks about our being "hugged" and "encircled by the mystery of God." Hildegard describes the Creator as "carrying" creation as a mother carries her infant in the womb when she says, "God carries us forever in the divine providence and does not forget us."[10] Time and again she invokes circle imagery for divinity: "Divinity is like a wheel, a circle, a whole, that can neither be understood, nor divided, nor begun, nor ended."[11] She adds, "God is as round as a wheel."[12]

To celebrate God as a circle is to deconstruct ladder-images of God that so readily legitimize hierarchical ladder-climbing in search of a God "up there" or a God "over others." Hildegard returns to the circle imagery often. For instance, she says, "Just as a circle embraces all that is within it, so does the God-head embrace all." Notice the embracing and sense of inclusion in a circle that's so in contrast to denouncing and top-down imperatives uttered from the top of a ladder. She continues, "No one has the power to divide this circle, to surpass it, or to limit it."[13]

Hildegard could hardly be more explicit about her understanding of the power of a circle versus the power of a ladder when she declares, "Now here is the image of the power of God: This firmament is an all-encompassing circle. No one can say where this wheel begins or ends."[14] The circle is all-encompassing. In this sense it's mother-like, embracing all. This is the kind of power God employs. Hildegard is proposing in clear terms that circle imagery be incorporated in preference to exclusive ladder imagery in our God-talk and our behavior. This is the Divine Feminine at work.

Hildegard also promotes what Newman calls "motherhood *as* theophany. Woman's primary significance in the divine scheme of things is to reveal the hidden God by giving him birth. In the meantime, she gives birth to this image in every child that she bears."[15] This is the *via creativa* in action, and it's close to Eckhart's teaching that we are all here to give birth to the Christ, "all meant to be mothers of God." In all our creativity, we are birthing the Christ.

Hildegard's multiple teachings on creativity are a celebration of the motherhood of us all. Our capacity to give birth and to become "flowering orchards" is an invocation of this motherly contribution. The same is true of her rich, deep, omnipresent teachings about wisdom and the search for wisdom, as we saw in chapter seven. Wisdom is feminine in the Bible and elsewhere. Where wisdom, and not just knowledge, is sought, there the Divine Feminine is being sought. The same is also true of the utterly democratic (circle again!) outpouring of the gifts of the Holy Spirit that Hildegard celebrates so often. The power of verdancy and creativity flows everywhere. It belongs to all. This too is the Divine Feminine at work.

Following Hildegard, her Rhineland mystic brother Meister Eckhart also paid homage to the motherhood of God. For instance, he asked, "What does God do all day long?" To which he replied, "God lies on a maternity bed giving birth." For Eckhart, like Hildegard, creativity was everywhere in the universe and the Divine Feminine was hard at work giving birth. Indeed, he maintained that when humans give birth, we give birth to the Cosmic Christ. "What good is it to me," he asked in a Christmas sermon, "if Mary gave birth to the son of God 1400 years ago and I don't give birth to the son of God in my person and time and culture? We are all meant to be mothers of God."[16]

Another of Hildegard's creation-centered descendants, Julian of Norwich, develops Hildegard's images of the motherhood of God in a most explicit and deep way when she writes, "Just as God is truly our Father, so also is God truly our Mother."[17] She echoes Hildegard's reference to being embraced, hugged, and carried when she says that "the deep Wisdom of the Trinity is our Mother. In her we are all enclosed."[18] Indeed, she says, "Jesus is our true Mother in whom we are endlessly carried and out of whom we will never come."[19] This is panentheism—the immanent presence of the divine in all things.

Like Hildegard, Julian celebrates Mother Earth and all her creatures when she says that "God is the true Father and Mother of Nature, and all natures that are made to flow out of God to work the divine will be restored and brought again into God."[20] Indeed, "God feels great delight to be our Mother."[21] She defines compassion—so important for Hildegard—in terms of mother love: "Compassion is a kind and gentle property that belongs to Motherhood in tender love. Compassion protects, increases our sensitivity, gives life, and heals."[22] Hildegard talks about our "being surrounded with the roundness of divine compassion."[23]

In painting our birth in original wisdom, Hildegard depicts a four-sided tent that comes folded up inside of us as tiny children, and she names the journey in life as one of setting up this tent. Psychologist Carl Jung, commenting on this painting, says that it took a woman to paint this fourth side of God—the God of Quarternity—because the fourth side represents the missing feminine. Interestingly, Hildegard in her genius paints the Trinity within the Quaternity in that same painting.[24]

In still another painting, Hildegard depicts divinity in four modes: A man sits on a throne, a ptah symbol representing the goddess from

Egypt surrounds the man, a large shell—such as Aphrodite emerged from—serves as his footstool, and a wheel of water holds up the entire scene. Thus she draws divinity four times in the picture, and three of the symbols are explicitly feminine. A shell relates to the moon and to Aphrodite who was born in a shell, while the waters relate to the fetal waters of Mary's womb. Hildegard refers to these waters as depicting "the abyss," and symbologist Cirlot reminds us that the Great Mother is associated with the abyss. Thus we have Hildegard depicting the Great Mother, the Divine Feminine. She democratizes God when she says, "Every faithful soul is a throne of God if it reverences God wisely."[25] We are all "cosmic centers," or thrones of God. Isis, the goddess of North Africa who is the basis of the Black Madonna in the West, means "throne" in the native language there.[26]

Healing: Mary Magdalene's Assignment

As we saw earlier, Hildegard is devoted to healing. From her music to her mandalas, her books on medicine to her books on psychotherapy or development of virtues to combat bad habits, much of her work is about healing. The historical Jesus was also devoted to healing. Biblical scholar Bruce Chilton believes Jesus bequeathed this essential part of his ministry to none other than his close friend, Mary Magdalene. Sadly, Mary Magdalene got very bad press in the 6th century when Pope Gregory mistakenly confused her with the harlot in the gospels. Because Mary Magdalene was entrusted with the healing action of anointing, Chilton believes she should be credited with the entire sacramental dimension of Christianity and its subsequent development. Cleary Hildegard is of that same womanly lineage of healing and anointing that later became clericalized and in great part restricted to men.

Chilton points out, "Rabbi Jesus conceived of divine Spirit, the force that dissolved unclean spirits, as *feminine*. From the time of the book of Proverbs (that is, the sixth century B.C.E.), Spirit had a firm place in Israelite theology as Yahweh's female partner. The force of Spirit that rushed out from God at the beginning of the cosmos and filled the entire universe was feminine both in the noun's gender (*ruach* in Hebrew) and in the life-giving creativity with which Spirit endowed creation. This Divine Feminine was closely identified with Wisdom, the eternal consort of Yahweh (Proverbs 8:22-31)."[27]

Chilton belies how masculine the Christian sense of Deity became after the Middle Ages, "since in Rabbi Jesus' mind, his whole movement amounted to an apostolic message from Spirit, and therefore from Wisdom... At the wellspring of his movement, male and female together reflected the reality of the divine image (Genesis 1:27) and God's Spirit conveyed the full feminine force of divinity."[28] But in Hildegard's understanding, this dimension of Spirit as feminine was in no way forgotten.

Mary According to Hildegard

Hildegard's Mariology is rich and deep. We should remember that the goddess returned in full force in Hildegard's century. The revolution that new Gothic architecture represented was a movement from the patriarchal, defensive, thick-walled soul of Romanesque times to the spacious, open, color-filled, tree-imitating, and soaring Gothic soul of the Gothic cathedrals. The very word "cathedral" meant the throne where the goddess sits ruling the cosmos with wisdom, compassion, and justice for the poor.

Henry Adams demonstrates the truth of the return of the Divine Feminine in this era in his classic work on *Mont Saint Michel and Chartres*. All the new Gothic cathedrals, so many of which came into existence in Hildegard's time, were dedicated to "Notre dame de Paris, Notre dame de Chartres," etc.—that is, to "our lady," to the goddess.

How did Hildegard celebrate the goddess who is Mary? We've already seen how she called her "the ground of being." She truly has a sense of the "Cosmic Mary" to parallel her "Cosmic Christ." Barbara Newman comments, "There is a strikingly impersonal quality in her lyrics: she cared as little for the 'personality' of Mary as she cared for the psychology of Eve. Both women are larger than life, not mere individuals but cosmic theophanies of the feminine; and the purpose of the feminine is to manifest God in the world."[29]

Newman sees in Hildegard's sixteen songs to Mary "the near-total absence of Mary as a person. She is rather a state of existence, an embodied Eden. Her flesh is the garden where God dwells; everything about her is joy, innocence, asexual eros. Her beauty is not that of a human form but that of intangible essences—light and fragrance and song... Nor does Mary have personal feelings or a personal history."[30] We might say that Mary for Hildegard is the archetype of the Divine Feminine.

Hildegard calls Mary the "sister of Wisdom," who makes creation even more excellent than when it began:

> O form of woman, sister of Wisdom,
> how great is your glory!
> For in you there rose a life unquenchable
> that death shall never stifle.
> Wisdom exalted you to make
> all creatures fairer in your beauty
> than they were when the world was born.[31]

Newman comments that the title "sister of Wisdom" echoes the Book of Proverbs, (7.4) which says, "Say to Wisdom, You are my sister, and call insight your intimate friend." Hildegard explicitly connects the birth of the Word and the Cosmic Christ with the birthing vocation of Mary:

> You are that luminous matrix
> through which the same Word
> breathed forth all virtues
> as in the primal matrix
> it brought forth all creatures.[32]

Here too we have hints of the Cosmic Mary and her relationship to "all creatures." Newman likes to translate the word "virtues" as "energies." In addition, Hildegard calls Mary "luminous mother, holy, healing art!" who has "indeed conquered death!"

You have established life!
Ask for us life.
Ask for us radiant joy.
Ask for us the sweet, delicious ecstasy that is forever yours.[33]

Hildegard calls Mary "Mother of all joy" and a "glowing, most green, verdant sprout."[34] This is goddess language. Can patriarchy absorb it? Or do we have here new (but very ancient) wine that, as Jesus taught, can't be contained by the old, brittle, leaky wineskins of patriarchal society or religion?

Mother Church as House of Virtues

Still another expression of the Divine Feminine found in Hildegard is her wish for a church that is a "bride of Christ, inviolate virgin, mother of the faithful." The fact that the church so rarely was this virtuous woman pained Hildegard and was the source of much of her prophetic outrage, as we saw in the previous chapter. The church she envisions is an eschatological figure: it's the future, a work in progress.

Newman points out that Hildegard preferred "this consummate form of Woman, who embodies the whole of redeemed humanity in union with God" to other images of the church such as the body of Christ or ark of salvation—or, I might add, a church triumphant.[35] She paints the church being birthed out of the side of Jesus on the cross, from the blood and water that flowed. The church "can be ravished by rapacious clergy and, ultimately,

◆

"Mary, Mother of all joy, ground of all being, a glowing, most green, verdant sprout."

◆

by the Antichrist himself; in her role as mother, she can be bereft of her children through schism and heresy."[36] It's to this defamed church that much of Hildegard's apocalyptic preaching is addressed.

Hildegard distinguishes between the "kingdom of God" and the church. She liked to consider the church as a building in the celestial city of Jerusalem. Naturally she was partial to this image because she herself built two monasteries, and also because Scripture talks of the house that wisdom built. Hildegard saw the virtues as the building blocks of the living and true church. Virtues are personified as the "people of God" or as the real meaning of church.

Taking the passage from Luke's Gospel in which Jesus drove the money lenders from the temple and cited the Hebrew scripture, "My house is a house of prayer," Hildegard says, "'my house,' that is, the human being 'is a house of prayer,' because chastity and holiness ought to reside in the human...[and] righteous judgments of wisdom and honor ought to reside in the human being."[37] To say that the human being is a house of prayer is a kind of ecclesial theology that puts people and their powers of virtue ahead of all church building projects and institutional agendas. For Hildegard, as for Vatican II, church is "the people." Institutional embellishments are to serve, not narcissistically attract power to themselves.

Church is meant to be a "temple of holiness and with the edifice of the virtues," in Hildegard's words.[38] Every virtue, Hildegard said, is "a luminous sphere from God gleaming in the work of man." Newman comments that these virtues are "not a personified moral quality but a numinous force" that empowers human action.[39] They are powers (*Krafte* in German). They are modes of empowerment. This is truly an ecclesiology of the "people of God," as distinct from an ecclesiology of power, privilege, or institutions.

One of the most important virtues for Hildegard, as for any prophet, is that of fortitude or courage. In a remarkable exegesis, she declares that "Christ is fortitude," and proceeds to refer to fortitude as feminine. She writes that "the virtues hastened to Fortitude in order that they would be taught by *her* and...because *she* remained in the fire of the Holy Spirit."

Fortitude (who is Christ) "said to the righteous ones: 'Ascend from virtue to virtue into Charity's embrace.'"[40]

Love requires courage. Hildegard admonishes herself to stay strong in the midst of battle and paints a picture of two columns that a mythologist explains as "an upward impulse of self-affirmation." In this image she's celebrating the choices we make "to hurl away the deceits of the devil. God hurls tempests on humans, who are fragile. We cry out, 'I have such great and heavy things weighing my flesh down. I'm not strong enough to overcome myself.' What do we need? We need strength."[41]

Another virtue Hildegard heralds is knowledge. The church, or Ecclesia, is also a "city of the sciences," a place of knowledge.[42] Her vision of Ecclesia follows: "I saw the image of a woman as tall as a great city, radiant from heaven to earth: her head was crowned with a marvelous diadem, and her arms were draped with splendor as with sleeves...she was all aglow with luminous brightness, and clothed in great splendor. In her breast appeared the dawn."[43] In a painting, she pictures the woman Ecclesia alone and without male priests around her offering the blessing of the Eucharistic bread and wine.[44] "Ecclesia as priestess," comments Newman, though Hildegard is quick to remind the observer that women couldn't be priests in the 12th century.[45] Says Newman, "What we see throughout the abbess' treatment of Mother Church is a consistent feminizing of ecclesial and clerical acts..."[46]

Still another virtue, Justice, or *Justitia,* is meant to be the heart of the church and its preaching. It's the virtue of Justice who says, "The Church was born of me through regeneration by water and the Spirit; and we are one just as God and man are one." Justice is the very origin of the church. We've seen how many times Hildegard talks about the neglect of "the King's daughter, Justice." But she sees the church "persecuted from within by her ostensible leaders." In a vision, Hildegard saw Mother Church with her face "spattered with dust and her robe torn on the right side, her mantle had lost its elegance, and her shoes were blackened with mud."[47] All this damage was done by clerics.

Wisdom and creativity give birth to moral imagination and therefore to "good works" such as virtues. Hildegard paints a picture in which there's a shining city, and the "holy stones" that constitute that city "are the holy souls in the sight of peace" who "shine like gold." Why do they shine like gold? "Because in good people wisdom shows its own work of splendor... Good works came down from God into people and are moistened by the pouring over of the Holy Spirit. Thus the faithful person produces good and sweet fruit and obtains the company of the celestial city."[48] Among the "orchards" we give birth to are the virtues, those powers or energies that expand goodness and create empowerment.

This is the house that wisdom builds, and it constitutes Hildegard's understanding of the church, "which is a mountain of strength. There I proclaim the work of justice and holiness," declares a man seated on a throne. Thus Hildegard is saying that our ultimate creativity is about building justice and holiness, which happens in the place of wisdom. The church is people who create justice, holiness, and compassion through their creativity.[49] She is defining church as people, not as buildings and institutions, people embarked on the *via transformativa* by way of the *via creativa*. In fact, people themselves are the *holy stones* of the church. The church says, "I must receive and give birth," thus creativity is at its core.[50]

In another painting, Hildegard depicts Christ as a sun, and the church as a moon that derives all of its light from the sun. She is realistic about the limits of the church's virtue when she says, "As the moon always waxes and wanes, but does not burn by itself unless it is kindled by the light of the sun, so also the church is in a journey of motion. Her children often make progress in an increase of virtues and they often fail in a diversity of ways."[51]

The church is on a journey, and hence "church" is a verb, not a noun. It's where justice and holiness are happening. In her painting of Sophia or Mother Wisdom and Mother Church, Hildegard depicts the church as a mermaid with scales like a fish with people in her arms. She wants the church to be fishing in the soul and elicit depth from people, wisdom from people. She depicts wisdom and water together, the sea and the Magna Mater, the Great and Ancient Mother of the Sea.[52]

Let those who canonize Hildegard of Bingen and name her a Doctor of the Church, while also clinging to their power, privilege, and hierarchical mindset of dominance over partnership, consciously doing everything in their power to exclude the Divine Feminine, beware. They are in for many surprises. The Wild Woman is on the loose! We have heard from Hildegard in the 12th century. Now she may be ready to thunder in the 21st.

Conclusion

IS HILDEGARD A TROJAN HORSE ENTERING THE GATES OF THE VATICAN?

Rabbi Abraham Joshua Heschel, who has written major scholarly works on the prophets, says the primary task of the prophet is to *interfere*. Is Hildegard returning today to interfere? To stand in the way of a patriarchy out of control in society and religion?

What do the Vatican, the Taliban, and Pat Robertson all have in common? It's what fascism and fundamentalism share as deeply held values: The fear of the feminine, and an almost paralyzing terror of the Divine Feminine. The fear of sharing patriarchal privilege with others runs deep.

I believe with Ralph Abraham that the explanation for this panic in the face of the feminine derives from the fear of the goddess Chaos who, in ancient times and before patriarchy took over from the goddess about 4500 BCE, was honored and integrated into religion and culture. The goddess Chaos was respected because creativity was respected, and chaos is part of all birth processes. But with patriarchy's arrival, there came a conviction that it was culture's task to control the goddess instead of integrate her. Myths changed. Now we hear of Marduk killing

Tiamet. Patriarchal religion took it upon itself to control the goddess at all costs. Ralph Abraham explains in his important book *Chaos, Gaia, Eros,* how in the 17th century science took over from religion to complete the job.[1]

But something funny happened to the project in the 1960s when, thanks to the invention of computers, science itself rediscovered the role of chaos in nature, whether in weather patterns or in the imperfect ellipses of the planets—in fact, just about everywhere. Chaos was redeemed. She was back, and science was now her patron.

As a young mathematician in the 1960s at Santa Cruz University, Ralph Abraham was one of the founders of chaos theory. A few years ago, he and I did a public dialog on chaos theory, during which he told the story of chaos in science and I talked about chaos in our lives—what the mystics call the *via negativa,* the dark night of the soul. How rich and fertile a time the *via negativa* is, and what a prologue it is for creativity—a preparation of emptying so that the *via creativa* can come to the fore. Believers everywhere are going through a certain chaos today, and indeed our whole species is journeying through a dark night at this time. Following the dialog, a woman came up to me and said, "I am a midwife. Nothing is more messy and chaotic than birth. There is blood everywhere. But out of the chaos, a new being arrives." This seems to explain why a goddess-based civilization, one that honored creativity, also honored the goddess Chaos.

I'm sure that in our dialog, I cited the great Sufi Mystic Hafiz who tells us all about the dark night of the soul when he says:

> Love wants to reach out and manhandle us,
>   Break all our teacup talk of God....
> The Beloved sometimes wants
>   To do us a great favor:
>   Hold us upside down
> And shake all the nonsense out.
>   But when we hear

He is in such a "playful drunken mood"
    Most everyone I know
Quickly packs their bags and hightails it
    Out of town.[2]

Spiritual warriors and prophets don't "hightail it out of town" when the going gets rough. They stick around to assist and to learn. Hildegard was such a person. She was a warrior prophet in her lifetime, and she's back today because we need her to interfere anew with the suppression of the Divine Feminine and the rising of Chaos-killers in the name of fundamentalist religion and in the name of the state and corporations (fascism) the world over.

We also need to break our sentimental teacup talk about God. The issues of our time, such as ecocide and genocide, militarism and sexual trafficking, are issues of injustice that will not be wished away. They are built on economics that benefit a few at the expense of the many. The failure of education is of the same ilk. All the issues of our day require strength and creativity if we are to resolve them.

Hildegard asks, "Who are the prophets?" She answers her question in this way: "They are a royal people, who penetrate mystery and see with the spirit's eyes. *In illuminating darkness they speak out.* They are a living, penetrating clarity. They are a blossom blooming only on the shoot that is rooted in the flood of light."[3] Hildegard has penetrated mystery, seen with the spirit's eyes, and spoken out in the darkness. She is rooted in a flood of light and life. Above all, she

◆

"Who are the prophets? They are a royal people, who penetrate mystery and see with the spirit's eyes. In illuminating darkness they speak out."

◆

speaks to the darkness of our times, which I call "the dark night of our species," as we are being turned upside down to shake out all the nonsense. She illuminates our darkness. The mystics teach that the purpose of the dark night is to *purify our longing.* How important is it today to purify the longing of the human race? What are we truly longing for? Is it worthy of our nobility? Why are we here?

If we are here to accomplish something that's good, beautiful, and just, one thing is certain: it can't be accomplished if yin and yang, feminine and masculine, are out of balance. It can't be brought about by exterior force or "power over" dynamics. It can only come together in a balance of the Divine Feminine and the Sacred Masculine. We have to integrate these energies in our own person, then in all of our institutions from religion to education, economics, agriculture, the media, and politics. This is why Hildegard is back.

As to religion, this is what I see: When Hildegard enters the well-guarded and thick patriarchal gates of the Vatican as Saint and Doctor of the Church, she brings many surprises with her just like the Trojan Horse of old. Hildegard and the convoy that accompanies her includes the powerful lineage of the creation spirituality tradition, coupled with her fierce commitment to the reality of the Divine Feminine in its various manifestations such as we have witnessed in this book. Among these are the following:

> as the Cosmic Christ or divine image in all beings
> as life and therefore as the goddess who is in all of nature
> as the "God within" of mysticism
> as the motherhood of God
> as wisdom
> as the circle that is divine power
> as Love, the Lady who "made everything" in creation an original
>> blessing
> as the democracy of the Holy Spirit
> as the omnipresence of creativity
> as the love of Mother Earth
> as the fierceness of the warrior
> as the work of compassion
> as "the King's daughter, Justice "

as the igniting of wisdom that we are all born with and which is
   feminine
as Wild Woman
as relationship that penetrates everything
as keeper of the creative fire
as a church that is *not* defined as hierarchy or an institution but
   as the lay people who themselves constitute the "living" and
   "holy stones" of mother church and are themselves "houses
   of prayer" and warriors of virtue.

Hildegard is sure to lead the charge, not only on behalf of the return of
the proper balance of the Divine Feminine and a healthy and Sacred
Masculine, but to sound the trumpet today against the schism in the
Roman Catholic hierarchy, which has replaced the teachings of Vatican II
with demands for blind obedience to an all-male power structure. I have
written about this reality in my recent book *The Pope's War: How Ratzinger's
Secret Crusade Has Imperiled the Church and What Can Be Saved*, in which,
among other things, I call for taking the treasures from the burning
building. Hildegard is such a treasure. Hildegard stood up to schism in her
own day, and now she's back to sound the trumpet in ours. As keeper of
the creative fire, she urges us still to put creativity ahead of blind obedience
and Christ ahead of religious poten-
tates and sick power structures.

Hildegard's letter to King Konrad III rings as true today as it did in her day when she predicts, "The Catholic chair of Peter will be shaken through erroneous teaching... The vineyard of the Lord smolders with sorrow. Times are coming that are stronger than those which have gone before. The justice of God will raise itself up somewhat and the injustice of the clergy and religious will be recognized

"The Catholic chair of Peter will be shaken through erroneous teaching... The vineyard of the Lord smolders with sorrow....The injustice of the clergy will be recognized as thoroughly despicable. And yet no one will dare to raise a sharp and insistent call for repentance."

as thoroughly despicable. And yet no one will dare to raise a sharp and insistent call for repentance."[4]

Hildegard has raised a sharp and insistent call for repentance. Many Catholics the world over are voting with their feet and going into modes of *diaspora* as they sense that the past forty years of church history have been a journey away from, rather than toward, the promises of social justice and theological freedom, lay empowerment and respect of conscience, deep ecumenism and sincere dialog, that were the teachings of the Second Vatican Council born of the spirit of the gospels. Out of this diaspora great things can happen. Hildegard talks about a "remnant who have not bowed to the feet of Baal," who will carry on the real work of the church.[5] Renewal of religion is after all an inner matter before it becomes an outer matter. It is, in Hildegard's vocabulary, about virtues.

Thomas Berry instructs us that "the dark periods of history are the creative periods; for these are the times when new ideas, arts, and institutions can be brought into being at the most basic level." This occurred in the Middle Ages in the West, and also in the 3rd century in China when a dissolution of the Han dynasty actually gave birth to a "period of Buddhist monks and Confucian scholars and artists who gave expression to new visions and new thoughts at the deepest levels of human consciousness," which allowed the Chinese to survive as a people and as a culture. Such movements brought alive the wisdom traditions, which "are not the transient thoughts or immediate insights of journalists concerned with the daily course of human affairs; these are expressions in human form of the principles guiding human life within the very structure and functioning of the universe itself."[6] Hildegard is such a figure, urging us to wake up and come alive.

I have learned that the Dalai Lama gave a speech in Vancouver in which he said that humanity will be awakened and therefore saved by women. If he is correct, then surely Hildegard is one of those women who has returned to awaken humanity.

With her passion and fiery spirit, Hildegard leads the way. She is a herald of a new spiritual consciousness who will not be ignored, just as she wasn't silenced in her day. All this may surprise ecclesiastics who have canonized her and named her a "Doctor of the Church," which she surely is. Are those who prefer dominating others to partnering with others really prepared for this Wild Woman who "thunders after injustice" and operates from the gut and not the head? This royal person who speaks out from the darkness and is prophet and shaman, ally of scientists and feminists, of eco-warriors and artists? Stay tuned. With Hildegard's arrival, surprises are indeed afoot! You can count on it.

Appendix

EMPLOYING SPIRITUAL PRACTICES IN THE SPIRIT OF HILDEGARD

Many people say that the East offers all the spiritual practices and the West is totally bereft of practices. I don't agree. I do agree that rich practices abound in the East, from yoga to Buddhist sitting and walking meditations. In addition, beautiful souls such as Joanna Macy have adapted many ancient practices from the East for our use, for which we are grateful. But I also believe that we shouldn't abandon Western practice or refuse to adapt it for our use. Following are some practices adapted in the spirit of Hildegard that I recommend for your consideration.

1. Hildegard, like all Benedictine monks and sisters, chanted the psalms daily. The psalms of course are the wisdom poetry of Israel, and they therefore fed the heart of Jesus. I don't recommend rushing through the psalms or saying certain prayers each day to complete a form in a prayer book. I recommend instead sitting with just one psalm at a time, reading it slowly—preferably out loud—and *stop* wherever or whenever

your heart is touched. Don't keep going. The purpose is *not* to get to the end. The purpose is to dwell on the insight, the word, the phrase, the image that stops you in your tracks. Dwell with it. Don't move on. Be with the word or phrase or words. Let what has stopped you work its power on you.

2. Hildegard's words are themselves psalm-like and poetic. Take them and do the same that you did in exercise one. Be with them. *Stop* when something strikes you. Don't just "think about" what has been said, but let it wash over you. Be *with it.* Be with the silence it evokes. Do not rush on. One word or phrase or poem may be plenty. These exercises can move you from meditation to contemplation. Be with the stillness. Be washed by the truth. Be present.

3. Go into nature and truly listen. Listen to the silence. Listen to what breaks the silence. Listen to the "small" sounds, the birds singing, the squirrels dashing, the leaves swinging in the breeze, the trees talking (yes, they do talk). Listen to the grass growing and the earth being both firm and soft, to the flowers exuding their colors, shapes, perfumes. Listen to the waters. Listen to the stones. What are they saying to you? What is the Cosmic Christ saying to you?

4. Do a sweat lodge. Listen to the spirits in the sacred space, the dark womb, spirit speaking through your fellow people at prayer, but also through the burning rocks, the prayers of the leader, the sweat of your body, your own prayers welling up, the pain. Be there. Do not think about it. Watch the rocks— they often take on shapes and have lessons to teach. Be grateful to the fire makers and those who prepare the sweat lodge. Listen to the songs and the ancestors who ride in on the songs. Pray for strength—and for joy.

5. Listen to Hildegard's music. You can find it everywhere today, usually with the lyrics included. But you can also find her music as instrumental only.[1] Listen with your heart. Listen with your soul. Ask: What is Hildegard saying to me through this music? Be with Hildegard and her music. Let it wash over you, refresh you, penetrate you, draw silence from you. Don't rush through it. One song at one sitting should be enough to cleanse and excite your soul.

6. Listen to and watch Hildegard's opera. Sometimes it's performed publicly. For instance, I've seen it at Stanford University and also in the cathedral of Seattle. Get the DVD that the BBC put together, a quality piece called "Hildegard von Bingen In Portrait, Ordo Virtutum."[2] You may want to watch it with your eyes closed, just listening to the music. Some people find the images, and even the translation of the words, interfere with the experience. Be with the music. Be with Hildegard. What is she saying that translates to today's needs? Her morality play is about virtue triumphing over vice—a not altogether irrelevant topic today.

7. You might want to ask yourself: If I were writing such a play today, how would I change the story and the lyrics? How would I make the movie today? Can I still incorporate her music in doing so? Rewrite the script, then get a cam recorder and try birthing your own version. How would Hildegard write the opera today if she were with us?

8. Practice creativity—practice art as meditation. Take up painting, dance, working with clay, journaling, poetry, photography, or moviemaking. Spend time with it *not* to "produce a product" but to enter into a prayerful process. Be with the colors and shapes and forms in painting; be with the clay with

its firmness and its wetness; be with your body, its muscles and sinews in movement; be with your running thoughts in journaling; be with your images and words in poetry. Make it a prayer. Let all these practices speak to you. Celebrate your creativity, your greenness!

9. Look about for other spiritual practices that might speak to you. Yoga? Zen sitting? Walking with intention on the sacred earth? Martial Arts? Tai Chi? Aikido? Bring Hildegard into your space when you do these things. Memorize one sentence from her teachings and recite it mantra-like as you do your meditation.

10. Chant Hildegard's phrases mantra-like. Pick a short phrase that speaks to you and chant it over and over. It's the rhythm, the beat that counts—*not* moving on to more chants. Depth, not breadth. The Now, not the past, the future, or the many. Quality, not quantity. Following are examples of some phrases you may choose to chant:
   Holy Spirit, life of the life of all creatures
   All is penetrated with connectedness, penetrated with
      relatedness
   Holy spirit is life-giving-life
   Holy Spirit, root of all being
   I am the yearning for good
   I ignite the beauty of the plains
   I sparkle the waters
   I burn in the sun, the moon, and the stars
   Trinity, you are music, you are life
   No creation without a radiance
   Be not lax in celebrating
   Mary, Mother of all joy
   Mary, ask for us life, ask for us radiant joy
   Mary, ground of all being, Greetings!

I have exalted humankind with the vocation of creation
God is delighted by humankind
The earth should not be injured, the earth should not be
   destroyed
Limitless love flooding all, loving all
Feather on the breath of God

11. Meditate on Hildegard's mandalas or other illuminations. Be
with them in silence. What are they saying to you? What deep
silence are they stirring in you? Which ones attract you the
most and why? What healing results from your time spent with
these paintings?

12. Take Hildegard with you when you work out. If on a machine
where you can read while you run or walk, put her words in
front of you; or put her paintings and mandalas in front of you
to inspire your meditations.

13. If you are running, lifting weights, swimming, or dancing
ecstatic dance, memorize a few mantras from Hildegard and
chant them as you work out. Ask her to enter your space, your
heart, your mind, your body. If you like to sing, sing some of
her melodies as you work out.

14. Practice honoring the Cosmic Christ who is in all things. This is
the essence of the "Namaste" bow of reverence in the Hindu
tradition. Salute, bow, and respect all beings, becoming ever
more aware of the omnipresence of the Cosmic Christ, Buddha
nature, Shekinah, or God-presence in everything. Your bow may
be explicit or it may be implicit, something you do inside yourself.

15. Find a leaf, a stone, a feather, or a small being of any kind and
hold it meditatively in your hand. Ask it to tell you of its story,

its being, its holy existence. Why is it here? What does it want to tell you? Where does it come from in its 13.7 billion year journey to now? Ask its permission before you discard it or take it with you.

16. Do gardening. Go to the earth; stir it up. Learn what it's made of. Plant something. Care for it. Watch what gifts it brings forth. Invite others to participate.

17. Support an artist. Affirm an artist. Learn the stories of artists and their spiritual journeys through their art. Look at art and let it speak to you. Let Spirit speak to your through the art whether it's painting, sculpture, film, poetry or theater. Ask it what it has to teach you.

18. Support the artist in yourself. Affirm this artist. Rejoice at the gift of being able to give birth, however difficult the process, however full of doubt or worry. Make creativity a priority.

19. Resist couchpotatoitis. Don't let your soul die on your couch in front of excessive television viewing—or from addiction to your computer and the internet. Get outdoors!

20. Protest! Write letters to congress, church leaders, news people and other media, and companies that sponsor the media, expressing your passion for values of ecology and justice of all kinds. March and join occupy movements.

21. Share what Hildegard does for you with others. Share her mystical love of cosmos, earth, and earth creatures, but also her moral outrage and prophetic anger. Use Hildegard to help burn through denial.

22. Meditate on this question: What does Eckhart mean when he says "God is the Denial of denial?" How was Hildegard a denier of denial? How can you contribute to denying denial?

23. Draw your own mandalas or healing circles.

24. Gather a circle of people to read Hildegard together and discuss her work, and to read this book. What is Hildegard telling you today?

25. Have this same circle listen to her music and/or meditate together on her illuminations. What are they saying to you today?

26. Send reminders to hierarchy and clergy of Hildegard's anger and displeasure at those who are intellectually lazy or "lukewarm" about justice.

27. Send these same people the list of Hildegard's Divine Feminine theology (see the Conclusion) and ask them when these teachings of a "Doctor of the Church" will be implemented.

28. Write the members of the Supreme Court—especially those who are Catholic and voted for "citizens united." Where in any Christian teachings are we told that corporations are people? Join those who protest such nonsense.

29. Make a pilgrimage to Hildegard's convent and the Rhineland area.

30. Consider with others the 95 theses for church reform and the "25 Concrete Steps to Bring Christian Communities Alive Again" that I lay out in my books The New Reformation and The Pope's War. How are we doing? How can we implement these actions?

31. Hildegard names elements we need to balance in our lives through developing thirty-five virtues in preference to thirty-five vices. Which virtues do you think you need to develop the most? How are you doing this? Which virtues does our culture most need to develop at this time? Which vices are most weighing us down?

32. Hildegard urges us to be "as strong as a tree" and to be "spiritual warriors" like Christ was. Recite these phrases as mantras, repeating them often. Go to a favorite tree or forest and recite them sitting in front of the tree. Expect to hear some messages as the tree speaks back to you.

33. Hildegard preached harsh lessons to clergy and wrote tough words to ecclesiastical potentates. Do the same. Write letters to people in Rome about what you think of their actions and lack of actions around the pedophile crisis and more. Write letters to editors of newspapers and call in to talk shows to give your same opinions. Find your voice—as Hildegard did.

34. Start new base communities or participate in the new base churches, often with women priests leading them, small communities to restart Christian prayer and practice. (See www.creationspiritualitycommunity.org.)

35. Support, lead, or participate in the Cosmic Mass movement to bring dance and postmodern art forms like vj, rap, and dj to worship. (See www.thecosmicmass.org.) Or the Ecstatic Dance movement. Remember Hildegard's teaching: "Be not lax in celebrating, Be not lazy in the festive service of God. Be ablaze with enthusiasm. Les us be an alive, burning offering before the altar of God!"

Acknowledgments

I wish to thank all those who have traveled with me on my journey with Hildegard, a journey that began over thirty years ago at the Institute of Culture and Creation Spirituality at Mundelein College, Chicago. I want to thank Meister Eckhart who led me to Hildegard, and Thomas Berry who was the first person I met who was conversant with Hildegard, together with his side-kick and Hildegardian enthusiast to this day, Brian Swimme. I also wish to thank musicians MaryLiz Smith and Mimi Dye who have committed Hildegard to music. Ferene van Damme of the BBC invited me to contribute to their putting together a rich DVD on Hildegard's opera, her life, her paintings, and her contributions, called "Hildegard of Bingen In Portrait: Ordo Virtutum." Gabrielle Uhlein wrote her excellent master's thesis on "Meditations with Hildegard of Bingen" with our ICCS program. The people at Bear & Co (now Inner Traditions) put many of Hildegard's works into the world in an alluring and timely fashion, especially Barbara and Jerry Clow. Ron Miller translated Hildegard's letters and provided excellent introductions to them for my book *Hildegard's Book of Divine Works, Letters and Songs.* I am grateful to Bruce Howzeski for his translation of *Scivias,* and Brendan Doyle who conducted the choir that sang her music at several Hildegard Masses and events at the GTU, Holy Names College, and elsewhere. Mary Ford Grabowski's doctoral thesis at Princeton University on Jung and Hildegard first brought us together. Susan Evens-Peterson envisioned a retreat on "Hildegard and the Via Creativa" in Boulder, Colorado, in 2012 that once again excited me about the need for Hildegard's voice today. I also wish to thank Jeannine Goode-Allen for her inspiring work and deep devotion to Hildegard, as well as my many other students over the years who were inspired and empowered by Hildegard.

I am grateful too to the many other scholars who have arisen since we first made strides in putting Hildegard into the world, with special praise to Bruce Howzeski, Beverly Mayne Kienzle, Barbara Newman, Priscilla Throop, and Dr Strehlow and Dr Hertzka whom I cite in this book. It's gratifying to see how many scholars are plumbing Hildegard's wisdom, but I also hope that they do their own inner work so that any reptilian-driven academic competitiveness doesn't outweigh the joy of sharing that ought to lie at the heart of authentic spiritual work and scholarship. In the given academic world it's often difficult to keep spirit alive as distinct from mere collecting of factual data, and it's a pity how rarely academicians nurture their mystical brains. We cannot afford such a lapse in studying our greatest mystical souls like Hildegard.

Appreciation is due also to Sister Joan Chittister for living out the spirit and the fortitude of her sister Hildegard and for so exemplifying a Hildegardian spirit in her own vocation. I especially wish to thank her for her rich Preface to this book. And thanks are due to Mary Oliver for her own deep journey of creation spirituality.

I wish to thank my publisher, Constance Kellough, for committing to the task of getting this book turned around swiftly for the Hildegardian event and her leading a quality team along the way, and David Robert Ord for his fine editorial improvements to the book. I am grateful to Mel Bricker who assisted with permissions and to Dennis Edwards for his support at Friends of Creation Spirituality headquarters, as well as Ron Tuazon for his support. Thanks go also to Aaron Stern and the Academy of the Love of Learning who support my work so that books like this are possible. And praise to Javier Garcia Lemus for his rich paintings of the Divine Feminine, some of which are viewable in Namaste Publishing's Fall 2012 E-zine, which can be accessed at www.namastepublishing.com.

Notes

Introduction

1 Cited in Matthew Fox, *Hildegard of Bingen's Book of Divine Works with Letters and Songs* (Santa Fe: Bear & Co., 1987), 308-310.

2 Bede Griffiths, *The Marriage of East and West* (Tucson, Az: Medio Media, 2003), 151-52.

3 Ibid., 199.

4 Matthew Fox, *The Hidden Spirituality of Men: Ten Metaphors for Awakening the Sacred Masculine* (Novato, CA: New World Library, 2008), 221-275.

Chapter 1

1 Beverly Mayne Kienzle, *Hildegard of Bingen: Homilies on the Gospels* (Collegeville, MN., Liturgical Press, 2011), 2.

2 Cited in Gabriele Uhlein, *Meditations with Hildegard of Bingen* (Santa Fe, NM: Bear & Co., 1983), 14. One academician has attacked this work as being unreliable, but nothing could be further from the truth. The author in fact is a German woman raised not far from Bingen itself, though she did not hear about Hildegard until she attended my master's program at Mundelein College in Chicago. So I think it can be safely said that her translating is reliable. Moreover, Gabriele Uhlein is a Franciscan sister, which means she has been doing her inner work for many decades—something that academicians are often not well schooled in. Instead of attacking Uhlein's work, I recommend more meditation to the academician who practically fulfilled the warning of Thomas Berry: That academia deserves to be called "barbaric" in our time.

3 I have laid forth my argument for the schism of the present and previous papacies (an opinion I share with other theologians) in my

recent book, *The Pope's War: Why Ratzinger's Secret Crusade Has Imperiled the Church and What Can Be Saved* (New York: Sterling Ethos, 2011).

4   See Kienzle, 2-4.

5   Uhlein, 47.

6   Bruce Hozeski, trans., *Hildegard of Bingen's Scivias* (Santa Fe, NM: Bear & Co., 1986), 395.

7   Ibid., 394.

Chapter 2

1   Uhlein, 49.

2   Ibid.

3   Ibid.

4   Ibid.

5   Ibid.

6   Mary Oliver, "The Spirit Likes to Dress Up Like This," in Mary Oliver, *Dream Work* (New York: Atlantic Monthly Press, 1986), 52, 53.

7   Uhlein, 47.

8   Ibid., 45.

9   Ibid., 24.

10 Ibid., 30.

11 Matthew Fox, *Hildegard's Book of Divine Works with Letters and Songs* (Santa Fe, NM: Bear & Co., 1987), 349, 350.

12 Mary Oliver, "At the River Clarion," in Mary Oliver, *Evidence: Poems by Mary Oliver* (Boston: Beacon Press, 2009), 51, 52.

13 Thomas Berry, *The Great Work: Our Way into the Future* (New York: Bell Tower, 1999), 190.

14 Cited in Hozeski, 382.

15 Ibid., 363.

16 Ibid., 351.

17 Ibid., 349, 350.

18 Ibid., 349.

Chapter 3

1. Cited in Luther E. Smith, Jr., *Howard Thurman: Essential Writings* (Maryknoll, NY: Orbis Books, 2006), 93, 94.
2. Howard Thurman, *The Creative Encounter* (Richmond, IN: Friends United Press, 1954), 28.
3. Uhlein, 28.
4. Thurman, 29.
5. Smith, 91, 92.
6. Uhlein, 40.
7. Ibid., 37.
8. Fox, *Hildegard's Book of Divine Works*, 138.
9. Howard Thurman, *Deep River and The Negro Spiritual Speaks of Life and Death* (Richmond, IN, Friends United Press, 1996), 27.
10. Uhlein, 32.
11. Thurman, *Deep River,* 75.
12. Ibid., 60.
13. Ibid., 94.
14. Uhlein, 28.
15. Cited in Fox, *Hildegard of Bingen's Book of Divine Works,* 129.
16. Ibid., 131f.
17. Ibid., 134
18. Ibid., 132, 133.
19. Ibid., 134, 135.
20. Ibid., 138.
21. Ibid., 135.
22. Ibid., 137, 138.
23. Ibid., 138.
24. Thurman, *Deep River,* [52].
25. Cited in Matthew Fox, *One River, Many Wells: Wisdom Springing from Global Faiths* (NY: Jeremy Tarcher, 2000), 56.
26. Cited in Fox, *Hildegard of Bingen's Book of Divine Works,* 128.
27. Ibid., 280.

[28] Ibid., 244. For more on the Green Man see Fox, *The Hidden Spirituality of Men*, 19-33.

[29] Cited in Fox, *One River, Many Wells*, 57.

[30] Fox, *Hildegard of Bingen's Book of Divine Works*, 139.

Chapter 4

[1] See Matthew Fox, *Illuminations of Hildegard of Bingen* (Santa Fe, NM: Bear & Co., 2002), 92, 93.

[2] Uhlein, 58.

[3] Ibid., 31.

[4] Ibid., 128.

[5] Cited in Fox, *One River, Many Wells*, 426.

[6] Dietrich Bonhoeffer, *Sermon on II Cor: 12:9*, in *Dietrich Bonhoeffer Works, Volume 13: London, 1933-1935* (Minneapolis: Augsburg Fortress, 2007), 402.

[7] Uhlein, 90.

[8] Ibid., 51.

[9] Ibid., 57.

[10] Ibid., 51, 52.

[11] Ibid., 14.

[12] Ibid.

[13] In Hozeski, 365.

[14] Fox, *Hildegard of Bingen's Book of Divine Works*, 231.

[15] Uhlein, 77, 78.

[16] Ibid., 79.

[17] Ibid., 80.

[18] Ibid., 87, 103.

[19] Howard Thurman, *The Search for Common Ground* (Richmond, IN, Friends United Press, 1986), 83.

[20] Fox, *Hildegard of Bingen's Book of Divine Works*, 64.

[21] Thurman, *The Search for Common Ground*, 83, 84.

Chapter 5

1. For example, Joel R. Primack and Nancy Ellen Abrams, *The View from the Center of the Universe* (New York: Riverhead Books, 2006) and their book, *The New Universe and the Human Future: How a Shared Cosmology Could Launch a Global Society* (New Haven: Yale University Press, 2010); Brian Swimme and Thomas Berry, *The Universe Story* (San Francisco: HarperSanFrancisco, 1992); and Brian Swimme, Mary Evelyn Tucker, *Journey of the Universe* (New Haven: Yale University Press, 2011).
2. See Fox, *Illuminations*, 48-53.
3. See Ibid., 54-70.
4. Ibid., 77.
5. William Hermanns, *Einstein and the Poet: In Search of the Cosmic Man* (Brookline Village, MA: Branden Press, 1983), 108.
6. Ibid., 94.
7. Kienzle, 55, 51.
8. Ibid., 55, note 1.
9. Ibid., 56.
10. Ibid., 130.
11. Ibid., 107.
12. Ibid., 112.
13. Hermanns, 117.
14. Ibid., 90, 91.
15. Ibid., 102.
16. Ibid., 95.
17. Ibid., 106.
18. Ibid., 108.
19. Ibid., 135.
20. Ibid., 90.
21. Uhlein, 111.
22. Hermanns, 103.
23. Ibid., 94.
24. Uhlein, 125.
25. Hermanns, 106.

26 Ibid., 89.

27 Ibid., 109.

28 Ibid., 107.

29 Fox, *Hildegard of Bingen's Book of Divine Works*, 347, 354, 355.

30 Ibid., 356, 357.

31 Hermanns, 94.

32 Uhlein, 65.

33 Ibid., 41.

34 Fritjof Capra, *The Tao of Physics* (Berkeley, CA: Shambhala Press, 1975), 68.

35 Ibid., 286.

36 Uhlein, 87.

37 Fox, *Hildegard of Bingen's Book of Divine Works*, 281.

38 Rupert Sheldrake, *The Science Delusion: Freeing the Spirit of Enquiry* (London: Coronet, 2012), 7.

39 Ibid., 6, 4.

40 Ibid., 7.

41 Ibid.

42 Ibid., 109.

43 Ibid., 111.

44 Ibid., 116.

45 Ibid., 117.

46 Matthew Fox, *Passion for Creation: The Earth-Honoring Spirituality of Meister Eckhart* (Rochester, VT: Inner Traditions, 2000), 59.

47 Sheldrake, 127, 128.

48 See Matthew Fox and Rupert Sheldrake, *The Physics of Angels: Exploring the Realm Where Science and Spirit Meet* (San Francisco: HarperSanFrancisco, 1996), 137-192.

49 Ibid., 166.

50 Dr. Wighard Strehlow & Gottfried Hertzka, M.D., *Hildegard of Bingen's Medicine* (Rochester, VT: Bear & Co., 1988), 143.

51 Ibid., 115-130.

52 Dr. Wighard Strehlow, *Hildegard of Bingen's Spiritual Remedies* (Rochester, VT: Healing Arts Press, 2002), 53.

53 Ibid., 56.

54 Ibid., 59.

55 Ibid., xi, xii.

56 Ibid., xii.

Chapter 6

1 I have laid this tradition out in Matthew Fox, *Original Blessing* (NY: Jeremy Tarcher, 2000) and in Matthew Fox, *Creation Spirituality: Liberating Gifts for the Peoples of the Earth* (San Francisco: HarperSanFrancisco, 1991) and in subsequent books on creation-centered mystics, the Cosmic Christ, and more.

2 Hozeski, xxv.

3 See Matthew Fox, *The Coming of the Cosmic Christ* (San Francisco: Harper & Row, 1988), 109-126.

4 See Matthew Fox, *The Passion for Creation*, 30-35 for more on the Celtic influence on the Rhineland mystics.

5 Ibid., 76.

6 Juan Mascaro, trans., *The Upanishads* (New York: Riverhead Books, 1999), 119.

7 See Fox, *Illuminations*, 159, 107.

8 Berry, *The Great Work*, 170.

9 Uhlein, 118, 115.

10 Ibid., 28.

11 Fox, *Hildegard of Bingen's Book of Divine Works*, 226.

12 Ibid., 222.

13 Ibid., 220.

14 Uhlein., 38.

15 Ibid.

16 Fox, *Hildegard of Bingen's Book of Divine Works*, 349.

17 Fox, *Illuminations*, 79, 80.

18 Ibid., 81.

19 The painting is in Ibid., 83-87 and I call it "Adam's Fall."

20 Uhlein, 100.

21 See Fox, *Illuminations*, 127-131.

22 See Ibid., 107-111.

23 Kienzle, 48.

24 Fox, *Hildegard of Bingen's Book of Divine Works*, 364, 365.

25 Cited in Jane Bobko, ed., *Vision: The Life and Music of Hildegard of Bingen* (NY: Penguin Studio Books, 1995), 66, 68.

26 Ibid., 69.

27 See Steven B. Herrmann, *Walt Whitman: Shamanism, Spiritual Democracy, and the World Soul* (Durham, CT: Eloquent Books, 2010), 46. Also: Steven B. Herrmann, "The Shamanic Archetype in Robinson Jeffers Poetry," Oakland, CA, 2012, unpublished ms.

28 Bobko, 74.

29 Ibid., 31.

30 Uhlein, 93.

31 Fox, *Book of Divine Works*, 275.

32 See Fox, *Illuminations*, 118, 119.

33 Ibid., 119.

Chapter 7

1 Clarissa Pinkola Estes, *Women Who Run with the Wolves* (New York: Ballantine Books, 1992), 6.

2 Ibid., 7.

3 Ibid.

4 Ibid., 8.

5 Ibid., 9-10.

6 Ibid., 317.

7 Ibid., 12-13.

8 Ibid., 129.

9 Ibid., 13.

10 Mary Ford Grabowsky, *The Making of a Prophet: Matthew Fox at 60* (Self-published, 2000), 70, 71.

11 Barbara Newman, *Sister of Wisdom: St. Hildegard's Theology of the Feminine* (Berkeley, CA: University of California Press, 1997), 160.

[12] Steven Herrmann, *William Everson: The Shaman's Call, Interviews, Introduction, and Commentaries* (New York: Eloquent Books, 2009), 94, 95.

[13] Priscilla Throop, *Hildegard von Bingen's Physica* (Rochester, VT: Healing Arts Press, 1998), 205.

[14] Estes, 75.

[15] Herrmann, loc cit, 2.

[16] Herrmann, *William Everson,* 105.

[17] Throop, 138.

[18] Ibid., 141.

[19] Fox, *Book of Divine Works,* 368.

[20] Fox, *Illuminations,* 105.

[21] Ibid., 33.

[22] Ibid., 35.

[23] Uhlein, 30.

[24] Susan Cady, Marian Ronan, Hal Taussig, *Wisdom's Feast: Sophia in Study and Celebration* (San Francisco: Harper & Row, 1986), 15, 17.

[25] Uhlein, 85.

[26] Ibid., 37.

[27] Kienzle, 88-90.

[28] Ibid., 92.

[29] Fox, *Illuminations,* 69.

[30] Matthew Fox, *Sheer Joy: Conversations with Thomas Aquinas on Creation Spirituality* (New York: Jeremy Tarcher, 2003), 248.

[31] Fox, *Illuminations,* 66.

[32] See Ibid., 158-162.

[33] See ibid., 38-42.

[34] Ibid., 69.

[35] See Matthew Fox, "Deep Ecumenism, Ecojustice, and Art as Meditation," in Matthew Fox, *Wrestling with the Prophets* (New York: Jeremy Tarcher, 1995), 215-242.

[36] See Matthew Fox, *The A.W.E. Project: Reinventing Education, Reinventing the Human* (Kelowna, BC, Canada: Copper House, 2006).

[37] Uhlein, 54.

[38] Ibid., 58.

[39] Ibid., 106, 107.

[40] Ibid., 110.

[41] Ibid., 49.

[42] Ibid., 111.

[43] Ibid.

[44] Ibid., 62.

[45] Ibid., 69.

Chapter 8

[1] Fox, *Hildegard of Bingen's Book of Divine Works*, 292.

[2] Ibid., 287, 288.

[3] Newman, 13.

[4] Ibid.

[5] Uhlein, 75.

[6] Bruce W. Hozeski, *Hildegard of Bingen: The Book of the Rewards of Life* (New York: Oxford University Press, 1994), 14.

[7] Ibid., 40, 41.

[8] Fox, *Illuminations*, 140.

[9] Hozeski, *Book of the Rewards of Life*, 53.

[10] Ibid.

[11] Fox, *Book of Divine Works*, 273, 274.

[12] Ibid., 274.

[13] Ibid., 275, 276.

[14] Ibid., 17.

[15] Ibid., 297, 298.

[16] Ibid., 299.

[17] Ibid., 322-325.

[18] Ibid., 303, 304.

[19] Ibid., 305.

[20] Ibid., 328.

[21] Ibid., 103.

22 See Fox, *Illuminations,* 122-124.

23 Ibid., 104

24 Ibid.

25 Newman, 98.

26 Ibid., 131.

27 Ibid., 130.

28 Bobko, 19.

29 Newman, 14.

Chapter 9

1 Uhlein, 115.

2 Newman, 187.

3 Fox, *Hildegard of Bingen's Book of Divine Works,* 308-310.

4 Dorothee Soelle, *Theology for Skeptics: Reflections on God* (Minneapolis, MN: Fortress Press, 1995), 43

5 Ibid., 50.

6 Ibid., 92.

7 Ibid., 49, 50.

8 Fox, *Hildegard of Bingen's Book of Divine Works,* 134.

9 Marija Gimbutas, *The Language of the Goddess* (San Francisco: HarperSanFrancisco, 1989), 321.

10 Fox, *Hildegard of Bingen's Book of Divine Works,* 146.

11 Uhlein, 21.

12 Fox, *Hildegard of Bingen's Book of Divine Works,* 148.

13 Uhlein, 36.

14 Ibid., 29.

15 Newman, 93.

16 Matthew Fox, *Meditations with Meister Eckhart* (Santa Fe. NM: Bear & Co., 1983), 81, 74.

17 Brendan Doyle, *Meditations with Julian of Norwich* (Santa Fe, NM: Bear & Co., 1983), 103.

18 Ibid., 90.

19 Ibid., 99.

[20] Ibid., 106.

[21] Ibid., 85.

[22] Ibid., 81.

[23] Cited in Matthew Fox, "Creation-Centered Spirituality from Hildegard to Julian: Three Hundred Years of an Ecological Spirituality in the West," in Matthew Fox, *Wrestling with the Prophets* (New York: Jeremy Tarcher, 2003), 93.

[24] See Fox, *Illuminations, 76-82.*

[25] Ibid., 73. See 71-75.

[26] See Eloise McKinney-Johnson, "Egypt's Isis: The Original Black Madonna," *Journal of African Civilizations* (April 1984), 68.

[27] Bruce Chilton, *Mary Magdalene: A Biography* (New York: Doubleday, 2005) 30, 31.

[28] Ibid., 32.

[29] Newman, 160.

[30] Ibid., 187, 188.

[31] Ibid., 165.

[32] Ibid., 163.

[33] Uhlein, 117.

[34] Ibid., 118, 119.

[35] Newman, 196.

[36] Ibid., 197.

[37] Kienzle, 177, 178.

[38] Ibid., 112.

[39] Newman, 17.

[40] Kienzle, 174.

[41] See Fox, *Illuminations,* 117-121.

[42] Newman, 203.

[43] Ibid., 206, 207.

[44] See Fox, *Illuminations,* 127-131.

[45] Newman, 214.

[46] Ibid., 229.

[47] Ibid., 240. 241.

[48] Fox, *Illuminations,* 139.

[49] Ibid.

[50] Ibid., 106.

[51] Ibid., 102.

[52] See Ibid., 100, 101.

Conclusion

[1] Ralph Abraham, *Chaos, Gaia, Eros: A Chaos Pioneer Uncovers the Three Great Streams of History* (San Francisco: HarperSanFrancisco, 1994).

[2] Daniel Ladinsky, trans., *The Gift: Poems by Hafiz the Great Sufi Master* (New York: Arkana, 1999), 187, 188.

[3] Uhlein, 126.

[4] Fox, *Hildegard's Book of Divine Works,* 288.

[5] Newman, 242.

[6] Berry, 9, 10.

Appendix

[1] For example, that of Mimi Dye who plays Hildegard's music on a viola in a CD called "Spiritual Songs of Hildegard" and is reachable on line or at mimidye@aol.com.

[2] This four hour DVD is available from Friends of Creation Spirituality, Inc. at www.matthewfox.org.

Permissions

"At the River Clarion" from: EVIDENCE by Mary Oliver,
Published by Beacon Press Boston
Copyright © 2009 by Mary Oliver
Reprinted by permission of The Charlotte Sheedy Literary Agency Inc.

"The spirit likes to dress up like this" from DREAM WORK
by Mary Oliver, Published by Atlantic Monthly Press, New York, copyright
© 1986. Reprinted with permission of Grove/Atlantic Press.

Poem by Hafiz from the Penguin publication, *The Gift, Poems by Hafiz,*
copyright 1999 Daniel Ladinsky and used with his permission.

Meditations with Hildegard of Bingen, Edited by Gabriele Uhlein, published
by Bear & Company, a division of Inner Traditions International, 1983.
All rights reserved. http://www.Innertraditions.com Reprinted with
permission of publisher.

Two poems by Hildegard translated by Barbara Newman from Barbara
Newman, *Sister of Wisdom: St. Hildegard's Theology of the Feminine, With a
New Preface, Bibliography, and Discography,* used with permission of
University of California Press Books, © copyright 1997.

About the Author

Matthew Fox has been working for forty years to recover the ancient and earth-centered creation spirituality tradition of Christianity, a tradition scholars now agree was that of Jesus since he derives from the wisdom tradition of Israel. Fox's efforts have included reinventing education through a pedagogy that includes right and left brains, the body and the body politic, and that brings science, art, and religion together. He founded the Institute in Culture and Creation Spirituality at Mundelein College in Chicago and after eight years moved it to Holy Names College in Oakland, California. His efforts have landed him in some trouble with the Vatican that silenced him for a year and then engineered his expulsion from the Dominican Order after thirty-four years, as well as from Holy Names College after twelve years. He then became an Episcopal priest to work with members of the rave community to reinvent worship using post-modern language and art forms, and of course dance (see www.thecosmicmass.org).

Fox then started the University of Creation Spirituality in downtown Oakland that pioneered a doctorate of ministry degree that bestowed spirituality degrees on people of all professions who are doing good work in the world (based on his book, *The Reinvention of Work*, that suggests all good workers are "midwives of grace" and therefore priests). After nine exciting years he left the university and prepared a two year pilot program with inner city teenagers called YELLAWE to reinvent education from the inner city out and employed methods of meditation and creativity at its core.

Fox is the author of thirty books on spirituality and culture, including two previous books on Hildegard of Bingen. He has been credited with ushering in the "Great Hildegard renaissance of our time" by Dr. Mary Ford Grabowsky, author of *Sacred Voices*. He was invited by the BBC to contribute to their four hour DVD that includes Hildegard's "Ordo Virtutum" and her illuminations or paintings. With scientist Rupert Sheldrake he wrote the book, *Physics of Angels,* one-third of which discusses Hildegard's angelology and its application to today's scientific worldview. Fox is the recipient of numerous awards, including the Peace Abbey Courage of Conscience Award, the Gandhi-King-Ikeda Award, and the Tikkun National Ethics Award.

Fox is currently visiting scholar at the Academy of the Love of Learning in Santa Fe, New Mexico and lives in Oakland, California (see www.matthewfox.org). His books, translated into 48 languages, have received many awards.

namaste

PUBLISHING

books that change your life

Our Service Territory Expands

Since introducing Eckhart Tolle to the world with *The Power of Now* in 1997 (and later with *Stillness Speaks, A New Earth,* and *Milton's Secret*), NAMASTE PUBLISHING has been committed to bringing forward only the most evolutionary and transformational publications that acknowledge and encourage us to awaken to who we truly are: spiritual beings of inestimable value and creative power.

In our commitment to expand our service purpose—indeed, to redefine it—we have created a unique website that provides a global spiritual gathering place to support and nurture ongoing individual and collective evolution in consciousness. You will have access to our publications in a variety of formats—including some available exclusively on our site—as well as a myriad of multimedia content.

We invite you to explore our authors, our blogs on health, consciousness, and parenting, as well as the timely guidance found in our daily Compassionate Eye blog. Enjoy the wisdom of Bizah, a lovable student of Zen, dished up in daily and weekly doses. And because we are all teachers and learners, you will have the opportunity to meet other Namaste Spiritual Community members and share your thoughts, update and share your "spiritual status," and contribute to our interactive online spiritual dictionary.

What better way to come to experience the reality and benefits of our Oneness than by gathering in spiritual community? Tap into the exponential power to create a more conscious and loving world when two or more gather with this same noble intention.

We request the honor of your presence at
www.namastepublishing.com